MEDITATION
FROM
THOUGHT
TO ACTION

MEDITATION
FROM
THOUGHT
TO ACTION

C. Alexander Simpkins, Ph.D.
Annellen M. Simpkins, Ph.D.

CHARLES E. TUTTLE CO., INC.
BOSTON ❧ RUTLAND, VERMONT ❧ TOKYO

First published in 1998 by Tuttle Publishing, an imprint of Periplus Editions (HK) Ltd., with editorial offices at 153 Milk Street, Boston, Massachusetts 02109.

Library of Congress Cataloging-in-Publication Data

Simpkins, C. Alexander.
    Meditation from thought to action / C. Alexander Simpkins, Annellen M. Simpkins. — 1st ed.
        p.   cm.
    Includes bibliographical references.
    ISBN 0-8048-3115-7
    1. Meditation.   I. Simpkins, Annellen M.   II. Title.
    BL627.S543   1998
    291.4'35—dc21

98-27437
CIP

Distributed by

USA	Japan	Southeast Asia
Tuttle Publishing	Tuttle Shokai Ltd.	Berkeley Books Pte. Ltd.
RR 1 Box 231-5	1-21-13, Seki	5 Little Road #08-01
North Clarendon, VT	Tama-ku, Kawasaki-shi	Singapore 536983
05759	214	(65) 280-3320
(800) 526-2778	Japan	(65) 280-6290
(800) FAX-TUTL	(044) 833-0225	
	(044) 822-0413	

First edition
05 04 03 02 01 00 99 98 97   1 3 5 7 9 10 8 6 4 2
Printed in the United States of America

Book design by Jill Winitzer
Cover art by Carmen Z. Simpkins

Photographs on pages 2, 10, 16, 26, 36, and 118 are used by permission
of the San Diego Museum of Art.

We dedicate this book to our parents, Carmen and Nathaniel Simpkins and Naomi and Herbert Minkin, and to our children, Alura L. Simpkins and C. Alexander Simpkins, Jr. We are grateful to all the brilliant thinkers throughout the ages, whose actions helped make this book possible.

Carmen Z. Simpkins's abstract expressionist paintings suggest mood, movement, and mysticism. Simpkins has been painting for seventy-five years. Her first solo show took place in Camden, Maine, in 1962 at the Broadlawn Gallery. She has exhibited throughout the world, and her works are in private collections in Europe and the United States. She continues to paint at her studio-gallery in Sebastian, Florida.

CONTENTS

INTRODUCTION

Many great philosophers have wrestled with the problem of how to bridge the gap between thought and action. Everyone's personal life offers examples of this concern. We have all failed to put our best thoughts into action at times, from an unkept New Year's resolution to unmet expectations for ourselves. Sometimes it can be difficult to follow through in action, even with the best of intentions.

Meditation offers a solution to this age-old dilemma. Through the practice of meditation, people around the world have found themselves able to follow through and do what they previously only dreamed about. Action flows, often immediately, from correct thought. Self-discipline comes naturally. People enjoy increased vitality, can resolve conflicts, and experience an overall feeling of harmony and peace.

How is such a transformation possible through the practice of seemingly passive mental exercises? Our first book in this series, *Principles of Meditation,* distilled and introduced meditation from its Eastern traditions and taught how to meditate. *Living Meditation* showed how to apply meditation to improve many areas of modern life. *Meditation from Thought to Action* helps you discover and activate your internal resources, to actualize yourself and to accomplish what you value through meditation. If you truly intend to benefit from meditation, you must be willing to practice it mindfully and sincerely, while being immersed in action, living your life. With sincere effort, you can accomplish your goals. This book offers a guide to the meditative Way.

Discovering the resources within your true nature, you may clear the way for going from thought to action. Mind, body, and spirit unify as one. This book can help you on your path to enlightened action.

ABOUT THIS BOOK

The philosophies in this book—especially Yoga, Buddhism, Zen Buddhism, Taoism, and Confucianism—elevate the spirit and expand the mind to light the Way. We have added Confucianism because of the way it carefully treats ethical conduct and action. Holistic Western psychology grounds Eastern philosophy in Western science, with fruitful metaphors and analogies for applying meditation to everyday life.

Part II teaches you the tools of meditation, both those of mind and body, and concludes with a series of instructions on how to begin meditating. The mental skills presented will add clarity and flexibility to mind, body, and spirit.

Meditation is not just about sitting; it is about life. Because action is the focus of modern life, everyday activity becomes the primary setting for applying these concepts. Part III focuses on issues that affect action at its core, what holds us back from fulfilling ourselves, and what can make things flow smoothly. Through meditation, you can overcome the barriers within to find yourself being "you," the way you most want to be. You will learn how challenges and difficulties can be overcome using this active philosophical approach. Meditation offers a new perspective that can enhance all aspects of life. It can help you follow your path with wholehearted sincerity, strengthen your spirit to handle challenges, live in harmony with your body to maintain optimum health, and resolve conflicts. Exercises throughout the book guide you in applying these insights to your life. We hope that you will create your own personal variations.

HOW TO USE THIS BOOK

Read over the instructions for each exercise once or twice. Try the exercise when the opportunity arises. Make time to practice. Please use what seems most meaningful to you. Feel free to vary the methods somewhat to make the exercises your own. When you understand the principles behind the methods, other applications may suggest themselves. We hope that your efforts will lead to enlightened action.

PART ONE

The Way of Thought

We shall not cease from exploration
And the end of all our exploring
Will be to arrive where we started
And know the place for the first time.

—T. S. Eliot, *Little Gidding*

If we search far back to the deepest recesses of time, we find ancient wisdom to guide us. Eastern philosophies of Yoga, Buddhism, Zen Buddhism, Taoism, and Confucianism offer a Way to experience life so that people function with more awareness, at One with themselves and their world. These philosophies were founded by dynamic people of action who took a firm stand and carried their beliefs into the world. The profound and long-lasting influence of these philosophies has guided millions of people through the ages to live happier, more fulfilled lives.

Western Gestalt psychologists have investigated the unity of experience with perception. Self-actualization theory explains what motivates us and how we prevent ourselves from doing our best. These theories all suggest that the source of our perception and experience is from within. Once obstructions to personal progress are removed, human potential is unlimited. Eastern philosophies can help us to eliminate these obstructions, clearing the path to fulfillment.

Arjuna with Krishna as His Charioteer (from Bhagavad Gita)
India, Panjab Hills, Guler
Opaque watercolor and gold on paper, c. 1820

1
YOGA: FROM METHOD TO PRACTICE

To the illuminated soul, the Self is all. For him who sees everywhere Oneness, how can there be grief and delusion?

—The Upanishads

Y oga is both a philosophy of higher consciousness and a system of practice that arose in India against the backdrop of Hinduism. Hinduism is a large group of philosophies, religions, and cultural practices that embraces a diverse range of philosophical positions. Without any founder or historically recognized governing hierarchy to determine orthodox doctrine, Hinduism has been described as "a federation of different kinds of approach to the Reality that is behind life" (Graham 1971, 108). Modern Hinduism embraces the principle that opposing views are just different aspects of the one universal truth.

By the time of Buddha, there were as many as sixty different schools of Indian thought contending over doctrine, which may be divided into two groups: those that recognized the authority of the

Vedas and those that denied the authority of these writings, asserting instead their own position.

Archaeologists believe that ancient civilizations such as the Harappa had been living in India since 5000 B.C. Hindu writings were brought to India by Aryan people who migrated from Persia and Russia about 2000 B.C. The four Vedas (the *Rig, Yajur, Sama,* and *Atharva*) are among the earliest surviving recordings of Indian thought. The best-known *Rig Veda* expresses spiritual knowledge in 1,028 lyrical hymns filled with praise for virtue and beauty as personified in nature. The other Vedas include priestly rites, prayers, rituals, and charms.

Later, between 800 and 600 B.C., the Upanishads were written. They include dialogues and essays that offer a profound metaphysical philosophy which resolves apparent inconsistencies within the Vedas and is expressed through a multitude of gods and spirits. The Upanishads describe an underlying Self or world soul, referred to as *Brahman,* that expresses itself in diverse forms and beliefs in the world. The Upanishads' philosophical conceptions about the nature of the universe have inspired European philosophers and poets such as W. B. Yeats as well as the New England Transcendentalists, Ralph Waldo Emerson and Henry David Thoreau. The well-known saying *Tat tvan asi* (That, you are) comes from a philosophical dialogue in the Upanishads illustrating the underlying unity of the universe with the individual by a series of analogies.

The *Bhagavad Gita* (the Blessed Lord's Song) is a later work, also very important to Yoga. Written sometime around the second century A.D., the *Bhagavad Gita* describes using Yoga to resolve an emotionally difficult situation: taking sides in an unavoidable war between relatives. A charioteer, who embodies the spirit of the god Krishna, inspires and helps the great warrior Arjuna through a series of contemplative dialogues about the value and application of each type of Yoga. Arjuna is thereby reassured. With the perspective Arjuna gains, he realizes a higher consciousness that allows him to transform the meaning of his task, so that he can address his duty wholeheartedly.

From varying interpretations of Hindu literature, six schools of Hinduism emerged: Nyaya, Vaisheshika, Sankhya, Purva-Mimamsa, Vedanta, and Yoga. Most historians consider Yoga its own school, yet the others all contain some Yogic practices. The Hindu concept of an unchanging inner unity in the universe can be identified with and experienced by training in Yoga.

THE METHOD OF YOGA

Of the universal mind each individual man is one
more incarnation.

(Emerson 1926, 2)

Yoga is a progressive sequence of methods of concentration that result in higher states of consciousness and a healthier body. Yoga was written down by Patañjali, a teacher who collected and organized Yoga practices into the *Yoga Aphorisms*. Historians date Patañjali's work between 200 B.C. to as late as A.D. 200. The aphorisms describe in general terms what Yoga does. Subsequent commentary and interpretation led to further development of Yogic techniques and philosophy, but all schools of Yoga refer to Patañjali as the authoritative source. Yoga includes methods of mental and physical discipline that bring people into harmony with the universal. According to Yoga each person has an individual self or a soul (*Atman*). God is expressed in nature as Brahman, the Universal Self, and in people as *Atman*, the individual self. The various Hindu deities are an expression of one

God. Atman, the individual self, is an expression of God in us. Realizing this liberates us from our finiteness.

The word *Yoga* comes from the Sanskrit word *yogah,* which means "to yoke" or "union." This is the thrust of Yogic philosophy and practice: to reunite the individual mind, matter, and energy with its source. Yogic methods of restraint and concentration can be adapted to many systems of philosophy in which higher consciousness is sought, for example, Buddhism and Taoism. One well-known example is "The Treatise of the Golden Flower," a Taoist Yogic text.

Prana (vital energy) helps link the individual with the universal. Like the Chinese *chi,* prana permeates everything and everyone. With every breath, we partake of this universal energy. Breathing in tune with visualization, meditation plays a central role in some Yogic methods. By controlling their breathing, Yogis master their body and mind, so that they can concentrate without distraction. Yogis learn to control involuntary functions such as heartbeat and body temperature and can perform feats of unusual strength and mind control that are impossible for people who do not practice Yoga. Meditation can have far-reaching and measurable effects, as Yogis have shown through the ages.

THE YOGA APHORISMS OF PATAÑJALI

Patañjali's *Yoga Aphorisms* direct participants through eight levels of practice, known as the Eight Limbs of Yoga. The first level, Yama, delineates prohibitions against immoral actions, guiding the Yogi in what not to do. Yogis must not kill, steal, lie, or be promiscuous. The Yogi is guided in right action, or what to do, at level two: Niyama. The Niyamas instruct people to be modest, tolerant, sincere, clean, and healthy. Together, the Yamas and the Niyamas function much like the

Ten Commandments, guiding the practitioner in ethical action. Level three, Asana, encourages practitioners to perform Yogic postures and exercises. Hatha Yoga has developed hundreds of postures and exercises to promote health and longevity. The fourth level, Pranayama, involves breathing techniques. Patañjali explains that learning to control inhalation and exhalation prepares the mind for higher levels of development. Breathing techniques can be performed in static postures and during dynamic exercises. Voluntary breath control, normally an involuntary process, helps link the mind to the nervous system (for health, emotional control, and concentration) and makes it possible to evoke altered states of consciousness at will. Pratyahara, the fifth level, is withdrawing the senses from involvement with external concerns in the everyday world. Pratyahara is accomplished by focusing disciplined attention and attaining self-control. At the sixth level, Dharana, Yogis develop the intense concentration that prepares them for the seventh level, Dhyana (meditation). The final level, Samadhi, is spiritual enlightenment.

Patañjali claimed that by sincerely engaging in the Eight Limbs, Yogis achieve supernormal physical powers like walking on water and flying through the air. He also believed that mental powers like telepathy and clairvoyance could be developed through Yogic practice. In conclusion, he states that the Yogi achieves "the establishment of the power of knowledge in its own nature" (Yutang 1942, 132).

MANY FORMS OF YOGA

Through the ages, numerous forms of Yoga have evolved. The most familiar to Westerners is Hatha Yoga, in which body postures, healthy diet, and cleanliness bring about higher consciousness. Raja Yoga focuses more on techniques of mental development that involve training and transforming the mind to achieve enlightenment. Gnani Yoga helps people recognize philosophically that the individual self is only a manifestation of the higher, Universal Oneness. Bhakti Yoga involves selfless compassion and altruistic devotion to others. Karma Yoga teaches that through work, performed with spiritual depth and wholehearted devotion, people can find enlightenment. Mantra Yoga, now incorporated in modern methods such as Transcendental Meditation (TM) and in Amida Buddhism, uses the repetition of a mantra to focus the mind, leading to higher consciousness. Through greater self-control, all forms of Yoga guide practitioners to discover a deeply enriched and spiritual way of living. Yogic techniques are found in Buddhism, Taoism, Zen, and even Confucianism, through the practice of meditation—the cornerstone of Eastern philosophies.

2
BUDDHISM: FROM PHILOSOPHY TO LIBERATION

The perfect way knows no difficulties
Except that it refuses to make preferences;
If you wish to see it before your own eyes
Have no fixed thoughts either for or against it.

—Buddhist scriptures

B uddhism is a philosophy that originated in India around the sixth century B.C. and continues to live on today as a worldwide religion. Whereas Christianity helps people to overcome sin, Buddhism seeks to overcome ignorance. The sources of evil and suffering derive from the ignorance we carry in our own minds. This realization is disturbing but also liberating because we can do something about it. The cause of our suffering leads us to the means for our release: our mind. In this way, Buddhism is both a religion and a philosophy.

BUDDHA'S STORY

Siddhartha Gautama, the founder of Buddhism, discovered enlightenment through meditation. He called this experience *nirvana*, a

Seated Bodhisattva
Chinese, Sui Dynasty
Stone, 581-618
Bequest of Mrs. Cora Timken Burnett

release that he knew could help all sufferers. He became known as Buddha, the Awakened One. He dedicated himself to showing others the way to enlightenment. From this powerful meditative experience, Buddhism was born.

One sunny morning, Buddha was speaking to a large group of disciples who had gathered around him, enthralled by his message. At the end of the lecture, Buddha held up a single flower and gazed out over the crowd. Everyone watched, mystified, except for one man, an ardent student named Mahakasyapa. A heartfelt smile spread across Mahakasyapa's face as he received direct insight, without words, into the essence of Buddhism.

Mahakasyapa became the dharma heir of Buddha. He devoted his life to keeping Buddha's teachings alive, organizing the First Buddhist Council following Buddha's death. Ananda, one of Buddha's younger disciples who had attended the master's lectures regularly, possessed an unusually sharp memory. He was able to recite many of the sermons word for word, beginning each one with "Thus have I heard," which is how all the earliest sutras open. The council worked together to verify the accuracy of Ananda's recollections, and the first sutras were transcribed and officially recorded. Thousands of pages of interpretations have been written down since. Translated from Sanskrit to Pali and now into many languages, these works enlighten people around the world.

Many sects of Buddhism developed, often in profound disagreement over the true interpretation of Buddha's words. Three other councils followed over the next several hundred years in an attempt at unity. At the Fourth Council, it was agreed that the two major sects could formally split and evolve in their own way. Today there are many forms of Buddhism, offshoots of these two original sects.

BUDDHA'S ANSWER TO SUFFERING

Buddha's enlightenment brought him insights that he believed could save people from their suffering, as he had been saved from his suffering. He formulated a doctrine for salvation that he called the Four Noble Truths. Illness, pain, failure, and eventual death are ever present. Buddha believed that life is not hopeless, because the cause of this suffering derives from our own thinking, through our mental interpretation. According to Buddhism, our craving for possessions, power, position, or other pleasures, puts us into bondage with suffering. It is our ignorance in believing these things are real and desirable that is the root of our problems. True happiness and freedom can come only through realizing the impermanence of all that we believe to be real. We must turn away from these desires, toward the higher wisdom that transcends suffering—a wisdom found in meditation.

We achieve this wisdom by changing every aspect of our life and following what Buddha called the Eightfold Path: right views, right aspirations, right speech, right behavior, right livelihood, right effort, right thoughts, and right contemplation. Buddha's teachings call upon followers to live a compassionate, moral, and aware life.

Early Buddhists sought to transcend this world of suffering (*samsara*) and attain nirvana by fleeing society, taking refuge in the forest to study and meditate. They followed the Four Noble Truths and the Eightfold Path strictly and with great inner discipline. These early practitioners, known as Elders, strove to become *arhants,* godlike living saints who dwell in nirvana and become perfect, superior beings.

In time, other Buddhists contemplated the philosophical implications of the doctrine and came to different conclusions. A dissenting group called the Mahasanghikas did not believe that arhants were perfect and godlike. They observed that arhants were human and imperfect, dependent on others. They argued that we all need other people and rejected the aloof and solitary life of the arhant. The Mahasanghikas developed new ways that evolved into a separate and new form of Buddhism: Mahayana. The Elders continued their traditional way, which became known as Theravada Buddhism.

MAHAYANA BUDDHISM

From its origins some 500 years after Buddha's death, Mahayana Buddhism has become a significant force. Mahayana Buddhism believes that the ideal person is the *bodhisattva*. The literal translation is "enlightened being," but in Tibetan, *bodhisattva* is translated as "heroic being." Bodhisattvas seek enlightenment, but unlike the arhants, they turn back to the world in compassion to help others who are not enlightened. This aim is stated explicitly in four vows that all bodhisattvas take: to save all sentient beings, to extinguish all passions, to master all dharmas, and to attain the truth of the Buddha, no matter how difficult it may be (Dumoulin 1988, 32).

The following parable from the Prajñaparamita Sutra (Wisdom Sutra) explains the rationale for such a compassionate commitment to others.

A man who had accomplished many great things in his life went on an outing to the woods with his family. While wandering through the forest, they all became lost. Wild animals threatened them, and poisonous plants were everywhere. The family grew very frightened. The man boldly reassured them, "Don't be afraid. I will find a way out!" Feeling no fear, he was able to maintain a clear mind. Resourcefully and courageously, he found the way out of the forest.

The sutra goes on to explain that, similarly, the bodhisattva does not abandon his fellow beings, but instead uses his own mind, filled with clarity and compassion, to heroically lead them to enlightenment.

Mahayana (Greater Vehicle) has remained a separate form of Buddhism from the Theravada, which the Mahayanas refer to as Hinayana (Lesser Vehicle).

NO-SELF

Buddhism takes a unique position toward the self, believing that it is an illusion. According to Buddha, the self is a source of suffering. In Western social theory, our individuality drives us to do things in the world; rational self-interest is a positive force that motivates people to make the world a better place: if it is better for all, it is better for each individual. Buddhists believe that self-interest leads inevitably to self-centeredness and will not ultimately make the world better. The solution is to base society not on the self but rather on no-self.

The Buddhist concept of no-self is that the self cannot be categorized, and lies beyond self or not-self. Buddhists point out that we limit ourselves by saying we can or cannot do something, we are not that kind of person. These concepts of self are false. We need not be bound by narrow definitions of ourselves. The self cannot be grasped objectively: the more we try to think about our self, the more we get caught up in illusions. The no-self of Buddhism can be experienced only through meditation: a mindful awareness that reaches beyond our concept of self to a more fundamental experience of who we truly are.

EMPTINESS

The concept of no-self is synonymous with emptiness. Buddha viewed the world as being in a constant process of becoming—one of continual change. Nothing ever is, but nothing is not, either. According to the Prajñaparamita Sutra, a bodhisattva should recognize that all things are empty.

Emptiness lies in the middle, between yes and no, being and non-being, always and never. Buddha taught that people base their views on two extremes: "it is" or "it is not." The truth lies between the two, somewhere between neither and both. Buddha believed that if you avoid the two extremes, you will find truth in the middle: emptiness. Thus, Buddhism is a philosophy of moderation. Buddha himself had been born into a life of extreme luxury and wealth. He gave it up to live as an ascetic, denying himself even enough food to sustain his health. When he attained enlightenment, he turned to the path between the two extremes, the Middle Way.

Nagarjuna, the famous second-century Buddhist, wrote a treatise on the logic of the Middle Way that has been studied by scholars for centuries. He devised a set of negations to describe the emptiness of all things without calling them something: being, non-being, both being and non-being, neither being nor non-being. Emptiness should not be misunderstood as a negative thing. Rather, it is meant to convey nonduality, i.e., *not* being two separate things. Later Mahayana theorists used the term *suchness* to mean reality such as it is, without superimposing our own interpretations. Like the modern empirical scientist who tries to describe reality factually without bias, the Buddhist attempts to look at the world as it appears in an absolute sense. Yet, the personal, relativistic perspective—though limited—is also the starting point for liberation. It is only through meditation, an act of our own personal mind, that we can free ourselves from ignorance and find true happiness. This is a basis, a springboard for action.

Mount Fuji Above Lightning (from the *Thirty-six Views of Mt. Fuji*)
Katsushika Hokusai, Japanese, 1760-1849
Color Woodblock Print, 1831-34

Bequest of Mrs. Cora Timken Burnett

3

Zen Buddhism: Wake Up to Enlightenment

Every day is a good day;
Your every-day mind—that is the Way!

—Zen saying from R. H. Blyth

Zen Buddhism has been closely connected with meditation since its beginning. In fact, *Zen* is the Japanese word for "meditation." The legendary founder of Zen Buddhism, Bodhidharma (A.D. 440–528), was an Indian Buddhist who is also credited with having started martial arts. The story of Bodhidharma, shared by Zen Buddhists and martial artists, has given both disciplines a spiritual foundation. (See our previous books *Zen Around the World* and *Principles of Meditation* for Bodhidharma's story.)

Bodhidharma expressed his dynamic personality in the way he practiced Buddhism. He showed his intense devotion to meditation through decisive action: he sat in meditation for nine years, facing the rock wall of a cave about a mile from the Shaolin Temple in China, never once deviating from this path. His reputation spread as the years passed. Hui-k'o, a student of Buddhism, heard of Bodhidharma's intense meditation style and approached the master, requesting to be taught. But Bodhidharma simply continued to meditate, ignoring him. Hui-k'o stood quietly and waited. Day after day, through all kinds of weather, Hui-k'o stood, awaiting Bodhidharma's acknowledgment. But Bodhidharma kept meditating. One stormy night, in a desperate act of absolute faith and complete devotion, Hui-k'o cut off his own arm and offered it to Bodhidharma to show that he was serious. The master was so moved that he finally came out of his meditative state and offered to teach Hui-k'o, who became the Second Patriarch of Zen. This legend should not be taken literally; rather, it is symbolic of how deeply committed these early Zen Patriarchs were.

TRANSMISSION

Bodhidharma touched many with his teachings, but none as strongly as Hui-k'o. Once Bodhidharma turned back from the cave wall, Hui-k'o became his devoted pupil. He questioned Bodhidharma about the Way, the Path to enlightenment. Bodhidharma told him, "All you need to do is meditate; this one method is fundamental for all practices."

Hui-k'o was surprised. "How can this one method be fundamental to all practices?"

Bodhidharma answered, "Mind is the root of everything, and everything derives from mind. It is like the root of a tree. All the leaves and flowers grow because of the roots. Without the roots, there are no leaves and flowers. If you follow the Way of the mind by meditating, then everything else follows."

Bodhidharma began teaching his intense form of meditation to the monks at the Shaolin Temple. But he found that the monks were weak; they continually fell asleep and had difficulty concentrating and keeping their minds focused. He decided that the best way to help the monks overcome these difficulties was to teach them through meditation in motion. He taught them the movements he had developed for exercise as well as to ward off wild animals and bandits on his long trip from India to China. These eighteen patterns, known as the I Chin-Ching, were the legendary beginnings of martial arts. The monks found that not only did their focus improve but they also became healthier! Thus, at its roots, Zen meditation was practiced in action as well as at rest.

Hui-k'o came to understand Bodhidharma's message on a profound level that transformed his entire life. The disciple devoted himself so fully to meditation that when Bodhidharma was ready to die, he gave Hui-k'o his robe and bowl. This gesture symbolized a direct transmission, from mind to mind, of Zen. Hui-k'o passed the robe and bowl to his student, Seng-ts'an, who wrote the first Zen poem, "Hsinhsinming" (Inscribed on the Believing Mind). Direct transmission has continued for generations. This method of passing along knowledge, from teacher to student, is still the way to learn Zen, even today. Books, lectures, and other sources are used as adjuncts only. Zen is communicated without rational explanations by direct, straightforward action.

Bodhidharma's new approach to training the mind and body stripped away written tradition and returned people to their own inner wisdom through meditation. His approach was not based on rituals or study like many of the other Buddhist sects. Zen enlightenment is inseparable from practice. Zen practitioners immerse themselves in meditation. They believe that theoretical speculation is distracting. Zen practice involves a complete oneness of mind and spirit. The martial arts add another dimension of oneness: the body with mind and spirit.

HUI-NENG: SUDDEN ENLIGHTENMENT

Hui-neng, the Sixth Patriarch, altered the course of Zen by introducing the idea that enlightenment can come suddenly, often when least expected. In fact, his own enlightenment had occurred spontaneously. One day he was selling firewood in the marketplace, as he did every day to support himself and his widowed mother. Overhearing a man reciting the Diamond Sutra, Hui Neng was so moved by the words that he suddenly became enlightened. At that moment he decided to devote his life to Zen Buddhism, and he did. He started a branch of Zen in which sudden enlightenment was encouraged and evoked by often highly unorthodox means.

Hui-neng believed that simply purifying and quieting the mind is not the Way. "Seeing" should not be passive looking. Looking is only the beginning. The Zen Buddhist *sees*. Seeing into one's own true nature brings about a revolutionary change in consciousness, a waking up.

For the Zen Buddhist, true enlightenment comes from the deeply aware mind. Sutras and teachings can only point to the way. The Way is more than that. Ultimate understanding must come from within oneself. There is no point in seeking answers from outside. Only through their own personal practice will people find enlightenment. Meditation is the Path.

Hui-neng's style of meditation was different from those of other Buddhist sects. It dispenses with all formalities and postures so that the mind is free to circulate—no clinging, no attachment. By sincerely devoting themselves to meditation, people will experience their original mind, their Buddha-nature, free and unencumbered by outward circumstances.

NO MIND

The nature of Zen insight is wordless, beyond any concepts that rational thought can conceive. It is experiential insight, born of emptiness. As in Buddhism, emptiness is not "nothing," not a negative quality, a vacuum, but rather more like open space, an opening, a window, a question. People in the West often fill each moment with ideas and plans, moving directly from one thing to the next without pause. But to the Zen Buddhist, it is the spaces between things—the emptiness— where greater truth lies. "To know that the mind is empty is to see the buddha . . . to see no mind is to see the buddha" (Pine 1989, 49).

With the emptiness of no-mind comes Zen Buddhism's Way, being fully attentive and unified with action, without thinking in worldly concepts about it. As Bodhidharma explained, "Not thinking about anything is Zen. Once you know this, walking, standing, sitting, or lying down, everything you do is Zen" (Pine 1989, 49).

WAKE UP: THE T'ANG MASTERS

The spirit of Zen teaching became bold, even wild, during the T'ang Dynasty (618–907) period in China. Wake up now! Be aware! The Zen masters made this exceedingly clear to their students in every imaginable way. They might answer a question with an irrational answer, a startling shout, or a sharp symbolic whack with a stick. All these methods were intended to bring about a flash of sudden enlightenment. Since enlightenment is an experience of mind, it can be transmitted directly, from mind to mind. Rational thought must be discarded for intuitive insight to shine.

Many stories of the seemingly strange interactions between prominent Zen masters and their students were eventually gathered for teaching Zen. Students meditate on these stories, which became part of collections known as *koans,* to extract wisdom. Even though koans are about individual encounters with specific masters, they reflect general principles of Zen. They can be best understood when intellectual thinking is set aside for the intuitive insight of meditation. The two Zen koan collections that are often referred to today, the *Hekiganroku* and the *Mumonkan,* offer a glimpse into the true spirit of Zen.

Huang-po was a ninth-century Zen master who believed that we must completely free ourselves of concepts. We must stop deciding between this and that. Only then can we find a state of tranquillity that cannot be shaken.

> A student asked Huang-po: *"What is the Way and how must it be followed?"*
>
> A: *"What sort of thing do you suppose the Way to be, that you should wish to follow it?"* (Blofeld 1958, 88)

> After asking many more questions the student asked, *"Why do you speak as though I were mistaken in all the questions I have asked Your Reverence?"*
>
> A: *"You are a man who doesn't understand what is said to him. What is all this about being mistaken?"* (Blofeld, 1958 90)

Zen masters used everyday actions to communicate that meditation can be practiced and enhanced with everything we do. Chao-chou (778–897) (Joshu in Japanese) is remembered for his spontaneity and creativity. In one famous encounter, a new student approached Chao-chou and said, "I am new at the monastery. Please teach me."

Chao-chou answered, "Have you eaten?"

"Yes, I have," replied the student.

"Well then, go wash your bowls!" was Chao-chou's answer. With that, the student was enlightened.

Zen awareness is developed through sitting meditation when one pays close attention to each thought and sensation, as later chapters show. Monks were expected to carry this awareness with them always. In everyday life, most people unintentionally leave their awareness behind, like the monk in the following story.

One rainy day, Nan-in was visited by a student who had recently passed his tests to become a Zen teacher. Nan-in greeted the monk and said, "You probably left your shoes in the hall. But did you leave them to the left or right of your umbrella?"

The student felt confused because he had not thought about where he had placed the umbrella. He realized that he was not carrying his meditative focus with him. He returned to study for several more years until he had obtained "every-minute Zen." (Reps 1980, 101)

JAPANESE ZEN: MEDITATIVE EXPRESSION

Zen eventually found its way to Japan, where the spirit of Zen took on a new character. The Japanese incorporated the Chinese Zen idea of intense meditation on life into the realm of action.

Dogen (1200–53), one of the greatest Japanese Zen masters, called meditation *zazen,* "practice enlightenment." There is no gap between practice and enlightenment: practice is enlightenment. Only by practicing Zen can you find wisdom. This is a more down-to-earth perspective. Enlightenment guides us in what to do and how to do it. But now we learn that what we do and how we do it can also help us learn to live enlightened lives.

If you practice zazen as a matter of course for many years, you will suddenly see the vital point of enlightenment and know that zazen is the true gate from which to enter (Yokoi 1990, 63).

Japanese Zen masters expressed their Zen spirit through the practice of what has become known as Zen arts. Calligraphy, poetry, painting, flower arranging, tea ceremony, and martial arts all became ways to express Zen enlightenment. Artists approached their work with intense awareness, so fully involved in each moment of activity that the Zen spirit revealed itself through them. The masterful expression of these arts provides enlightened insight, beyond words and concepts. The insight comes through immersion, not from outside. Some of these arts are explained more fully later in the book. They are the classical expressions of Zen but need not be the only ones.

4

CONFUCIANISM: CARING ABOUT WHAT YOU DO

*The Way of the superior person has its simple
beginnings in the relation between man and woman,
but in its utmost reaches, it is clearly seen in heaven
and on earth.*

—Doctrine of the Mean

C onfucian philosophy has had a profound effect on the East. It has shaped Chinese culture, politics, and personal life for more than a millennium. Although the principles of this philosophy existed even before him (as he readily admits), K'ung Fu-tzu, or Confucius as he is known in the West, was the first to coalesce them into systematic teachings. His loyal disciples and descendants carried his message forward and, forging ahead, made Confucianism the important force it is today.

At the time of Confucius' birth, in 551 B.C., China was unstable, with more than thirteen major and many more smaller kingdoms, all vying for power and influence. Confucius always loved knowledge and pursued learning with great enthusiasm. But his other great love, which he carried throughout his life, was music. He believed that music had the power to soothe the soul and bring harmonious

Fish as a symbol was often associated with Confucianism
Carp
Ganhi, Japanese, flourished late 18th century
Ink on silk, n.d.
Gift of Captain and Mrs. A. W. Borsum

relations among mankind. He said, "It is impossible for a vicious man to be a good musician" (Beck 1928, 238).

Confucius held several state appointments in his home area of Lu and advised neighboring kingdoms in protocol. He married and had a son, Li. But his main commitments throughout his life were formulating his philosophy and developing his music. He started teaching people in his home; many of his disciples faithfully stayed with him for the rest of his life. His reputation as an advisor grew.

He was given an appointment as minister of justice in Lu. Confucius advised the rulers to set a good example. He thought that doing so would encourage the same behavior in the people. Because of political turmoil, Confucius' advice was not put into practice by rulers until much later. Confucianism eventually spread far beyond the borders of China, to Japan and Korea. For example, Prince Shotoku of Japan followed these guidelines, setting a moral example with his own actions.

Confucius became so renowned for fostering loyalty and good faith, as well as for preventing dishonesty among the people of Lu, that the neighboring kingdoms felt threatened. Ministers from the nearby kingdom of Ch'i created a scheme to deflate Confucian influence on Lu by presenting its ruling prince with a gift of 80 beautiful girls and 120 horses. The prince was so distracted by these seductive presents that he neglected his affairs of state, ignoring Confucius' guidance. Disillusioned and depressed, Confucius left Lu. He traveled for thirteen years (497–84 B.C.) and was met with respect wherever he went. He never again aligned himself with any one kingdom, although he did often advise rulers on government, ceremony, and philosophy. His disciples traveled with him, always remaining devoted to their master.

Confucius finally returned to his native Lu in 484 B.C. and remained there until 478 B.C. In the final year of Confucius' life, the prince of Ch'i was killed. Confucius felt that the prince of Lu should punish the murderer even though the crime had not taken place in Lu. However, the prince protested that Lu was a weaker state than Ch'i and refused to take action. Confucius left, even more bitter and disappointed. As he was dying, he expressed his disillusionment with the political scene of his day. "No intelligent monarch arises; there is not one in the kingdom that will make me his master. My time has come to die" (Legge 1971, 87). Confucius never imagined the enormous transformative impact that his teachings would have on the world.

Some views hold that the original disciples of Confucius gathered after his death to write down his teachings in a book called the *Analects*. It is also possible that the *Analects* were written by later generations. *The Great Learning* and *Doctrine of the Mean* have been attributed to Confucius' grandson, Tse-sze, also known as K'ung Chi (492–431 B.C.), who hoped to preserve his grandfather's wisdom for all time. These works combine Confucius' interpretations with those of his disciples and remain consistent with the Confucian perspective.

CLASSICAL CONFUCIANISM

The basis for the Way of Confucius is through absolute sincerity; it is the beginning and end of all things. "Hold faithfulness and sincerity as first principles" (Legge 1971, 141).

Confucius believed that *chung,* or the golden mean—which refers to centrality, equilibrium, and morality—should be the compass for harmony and good conduct on the path of life. The mean relies on sincerity and being faithful to what is true, genuine, and authentic. Full self-awareness, with no deception, leads to a sincere will. By putting defensiveness and negative feelings such as worry, anger, fear, or even fondness into perspective, they will not interfere with the proper functioning of the mind.

CONFUCIAN MEDITATION

The Great Learning explains that the individual mind must be at peace in order to solve the world's problems. Meditation techniques are not explicit in Confucianism as they are in Zen, Buddhism, and Taoism, yet Confucius did believe that the inner mind is the root of everything. The following passage from *The Great Learning* addresses meditation:

The point where to rest being determined, a calm unperturbedness may be attained to. To that calmness there will succeed a tranquil repose. In that repose there may be careful deliberation and that deliberation will be followed by the attainment of the desired end (Legge, 1971 356).

A clear mind in meditative calmness is the basis for careful and accurate thinking. Only then does correct action follow. There are three fundamental life goals in Confucianism: to develop a clear character, to foster universal benevolence, and to pursue the highest good. These goals can be reached by extending knowledge through investigating things deeply.

The chain of reasoning of *The Great Learning* is that as the heart becomes sincere, the mind in turn becomes clear and calm. A personal life can then develop in the best possible way. Family life will thereby improve, and this harmony extends to others so that the state will be put in order, and finally peace is established throughout the world. World peace and order can be traced back through an interlinked chain to the transformation that takes place within the mind of the individual person. Each individual's calm meditation is ultimately the key to transforming the world. "Things have their root and their branches. Affairs have their end and their beginning" (Legge 1971, 357).

CONFUCIAN HUMANISM

From the Son of Heaven down to the mass of the people, all must consider the cultivation of the person the root of everything besides (Legge, 1971 359).

Confucius has been called one of the first humanists. He believed that people should be true to themselves. "Being true to oneself is the law of God. To try to be true to oneself is the law of man" (Yutang 1942, 122). The key is true knowledge, brought about through learning with deep understanding. Pursue whatever you do until you master it completely.

THE FIVE RELATIONSHIPS

Confucianism became a system of national orderliness and hierarchy, in which all people had their place and function within the system. The divisions were purely functional, not based on aristocratic birth or familial privilege. In classical Confucianism, anyone could become a king. Everyone should correctly play the part given them within the social order, and changes in status followed based on merit. However, over time, a system of static privileged hierarchy took precedence.

There are five key concepts in classical Confucianism: *Jen, chu-tse, li, te,* and *wen* (Parulski 1976, 31–32). *Jen* means "Man," the benevolence, love, and compassion among people. The allness we would be one with is expressed in correct relationships with other people. It transcends even death. Within the family hierarchy, the ancestors were respected; social, business, and family life decisions were made so as to please them.

Chu-tse, the superior person, the gentleman or aristocrat, follows the Way of virtue. People need not be nobly born to be noble: nobility is expressed by action. Anyone can do so. If a minister does not act nobly, he is not noble. In classical Confucianism, nobility is not merely a function of wealth, position, or caste: we are noble or not, from what we do. The ideal person, then, harmonizes *jen* with *chu-tse.* Sincerity and authenticity play a part. Mencius went even further than

Confucius. Mencius stated that if a king acted in an unfit manner, the people had a right to remove him from the throne because he had lost the mandate of heaven to rule.

Li, meaning both propriety and ritual, involves living by the mean, the Way of central harmony, the Middle Way, through customs, rituals, rules, and norms. Ritual is a ceremonial part of the ordered life, guiding action and conduct, and thus can be used as a basis for ethical, respectful, and cooperative social interaction. *Li* was originally dominated by the ritual and etiquette of the aristocracy. Confucius broadened ritual to encompass social and moral propriety practiced with sincerity.

> Leaders should be moral examples themselves. The leader is like the wind, the people the grass. Grass bends under the winds of benevolence and virtue. If the people fall into evil ways, look to the rulers for the reasons (Hucker, 1975 79).

Te leads to control and power through virtue. Whereas in Taoism virtue is found in living according to the mysterious Tao, beyond the everyday, as a guide to action, Confucianism believes that the correct behavior of each individual toward one another in the everyday world leads to central harmony and peace for all people. Truth is also moral truth.

Wen means the arts of peace, including music. Music, poetry, all arts, enable the listener to synchronize with nature. The arts of *wen* express the Way of humility, moderation, and restraint of the senses. *Wen* helps us to be sincere and wholehearted: to listen as well as hear, to look as well as see, to feel as well as touch. Perception is active, not detached. Harmony in music is symbolic of harmony in spirit. The universe is like a beautiful, harmonious symphony. According to Confucius, "Music in the soul can be heard by all the universe" (Parulski 1976, 33).

The five relationships are to be observed and the rules of propriety followed on the path to becoming a superior person. Father-son, older brother–younger brother, husband-wife, elder-younger, ruler-subject: these five relationships of respect and honor transcend even death.

Ancestors dead for three hundred years should still be respected and treated as elders. This principle, known as filial piety, became a central value in China and later in Japan. Confucius believed that the ways of the ancestors were noble and that their best intentions should be emulated and respected. Confucians are concerned that people always try to act according to what is correct, to be ethical, to seek the best in one's own nature. The Confucian follower seeks to actually do what is correct and ethical, not merely contemplate the meaning of actions. Only by putting philosophy into practice in everyday life can virtue be made real.

MENCIUS

Confucius' ideas were furthered and codified by his disciples, including his grandson, Tse-sze. Mencius was the next important Confucian to carry on the teachings.

Mencius (Latinized from Meng-tzu) was born in 371 B.C. in the same area as Confucius, the state of Lu. He lived in a time when much of the civilized world was concerned with raising the human mind, the time of Plato and Aristotle.

Chinese literature recognizes that Mencius' mother, Chang-shi, was a remarkable woman. His father died when he was three, leaving Mencius and his mother poor and alone. First they moved to a house near a graveyard. Mencius, being an adventurous child, liked to go there and act out funerals. Chang-shi said, "This is no place for my son," and so they moved. The next house was near a marketplace. Mencius went outside and pretended to buy and sell. She said, "This is no place for my son." Finally they moved close to a school. Little Mencius acted out the rituals of scholars. His mother said, "At last, the right environment," and they settled there. There are many such stories about Mencius' sensitive and careful upbringing.

Like Confucius before him, Mencius was disturbed by the corruption, civil wars, and lack of morality that were prevalent during his lifetime. Confucian wisdom seemed to have been forgotten. "Every man for himself" was common. Mencius decided to devote his life to virtue, learning, and influencing princes. Unfortunately, he met with the same resistance as had Confucius in trying to change the political climate. Discouraged, Mencius said, "Heaven does not yet wish that the empire should rejoice in tranquillity and good government." He withdrew from public life.

Mencius believed that human beings' spirituality must be nourished and cultivated, like a tree or a plant. The reason that some people become great and some become small is that the small ones follow their small tendencies, while the great ones follow their great tendencies. Both tendencies are within us all, but contemplation makes it possible to choose. Either the nobler or lesser aspect of things is perceived, depending upon the mind's capacity to discern the underlying true principles. The material aspect of things can delude and seduce us all, unless we combine correct thought with our sensory experience. If we do not look for deeper principles behind or within what is experienced, we may remain on the superficial, material level. The key lies within the human mind.

Mencius believed that the wellspring of virtue is the human heart itself and that innate goodness, if followed, leads to appropriate conduct.

The four natural endowments—commiseration, shame and dislike, respect and reverence, and feelings of right and wrong—are the basis for humanity, righteousness, propriety, and wisdom. They lead to moral consciousness, an innate feeling for the good. Virtue is hardwired in all of us. The true nature of humanity is good. Be sincere, be in accord with your true inner nature—the rest will follow. What is correct, genuine, and true guides us in how to be a good person, and thereby in developing our highest potential. The gentleman should seek to take action that is proper, to do what is correct and ethically highest. *Specific actions* are the focus in the real world, not just intellectual ideals. Mencius gave specific criteria for what to do. He also believed that if positive spiritual morale is maintained, proper conduct follows.

TSUN TZU

Tsun Tzu (298–238 B.C.) was the last important theorist of the classical Confucian school. He lived during the warring states period in China, a time much like that of Confucius and Mencius. He devoted his life to teaching philosophy.

Confucian views on the inner nature of humanity varied, depending on historical events and the philosopher. Confucius and Mencius assumed that our true nature is always good. Tsun Tzu believed that human nature is essentially evil, filled with contradictory and negative impulses. Outer behavior and conduct can be improved by education: virtue can be taught. The purpose of teaching virtue is not just to acquire knowledge but also to influence conduct for the better. Only through training toward the good can people become good. This issue is important: all the Confucians taught that whether people are inherently good or bad, they can become good through what they do and how they live. Education and social improvement programs are rationalized on the belief that behavior can be changed for the better; learning is possible and worthwhile.

Tsun Tzu also wrote a treatise on clarifying definitions, distinguishing between concepts by rectifying the names of things. Confucius had rectified names to preserve social classes, but Tsun Tzu took it into the realm of logic. He believed that if people used exact words (names) to refer to things, they could clarify understanding of their world. Unlike Taoists and Buddhists, who believe words deceive us, Tsun Tzu said that words do not take us away from truth. Language is an important tool to help clarify reality, so long as our words accurately reflect real objects. He urged people not to mistake the name or concept for the thing itself. "Names have no correctness of their own" (Tsun Tzu in Chan 1963, 126). It is up to people to create concepts that match their experience of the world and then use them wisely.

Confucius believed that innate human nature is potentially good. Mencius believed that it was actually good. Tsun Tzu thought that human nature is evil; only actions could be good. But they all agreed that learning and education would, through practice, result in better conduct and behavior. Better human relationships express higher human potential that would ultimately transform the world, bringing about peace and harmony. Confucians focus on what people are actually doing, now. Their fervent wish is that everyone do whatever they are doing better, with all their heart.

*Flowers and Bamboo
Around a Rock*
Chinese, late
Ming Dynasty-early
Ch'ing Dynasty
Ink and color on silk,
17th century
Gift of Mrs. John H. Fox

5
TAOISM:
THE NATURAL WAY IS
THE CORRECT WAY

The Tao is hidden and nameless
Yet Tao alone supports all things and brings them to
fulfillment.
　　　　　　　—*Tao Te Ching,* Book XLI, translated by Waley

Taoism is a Chinese philosophy that has had a profound effect on the world. Taoism's recorded origins date from the Chou period, 500-221 B.C., known as the Golden Age of Chinese philosophy. After centuries of developing and evolving, Taoism was firmly implanted into the spirit of China when Buddhism arrived much later, in A.D. 100.

Two individuals are especially well known as legendary founders and propagators of classical Taoism: Lao-tzu and Chuang-tzu. Lao-tzu used mystery and analogy, intriguingly ambiguous prose that conveyed the sense of the mysterious with its power. His book, the *Tao Te Ching,* is short but one of the most widely interpreted and translated books of all time. According to Eastern scholar Holmes Welch, no book except the Bible has been translated into English more times than the *Tao Te Ching.* Chuang-tzu communicated his philosophy through stories and anecdotes that not only explain what Taoism is but also show what it is not, by contrasting it with other philosophies. Confucius was his favorite foil.

LAO-TZU

Although historians debate whether Lao-tzu was a real person, his spirit lives on through myths, legends, and the ideas expressed in the *Tao Te Ching*. Perhaps Lao-tzu would have been pleased by the mystery surrounding him and his work.

Lao-tzu was said to have been born in 604 B.C. when his mother leaned against a plum tree and gave birth to a child who had been conceived sixty-two years earlier! He was born with white hair, so the people named him Old Boy, Lao-tzu.

Lao-tzu reputedly kept the archives for the Chou Dynasty in the capital city of Loyang. People came to him to study, even though Lao-tzu did not deliberately start his own school. Stories reported in Chuang-tzu's Taoist books describe several meetings between Lao-tzu and Confucius, who was fifty years younger than Lao-tzu and was profoundly impressed with Lao-tzu's wisdom. Confucius was said to have remarked after leaving Lao-tzu, "I understand many things about life, but when it comes to dragons, I do not understand how they can fly. Lao-tzu is like the dragon."

At the ripe age of 160, Lao-tzu decided to leave behind the corruption of the city. As he passed through the city gates, he left a short statement of his beliefs, the *Tao Te Ching*. Lao-tzu was never seen again, although some say that he went to India to convert the Buddha. That these stories live on after so many centuries is a powerful reminder to us all of how meaningful Lao-tzu's message has been to so many for so long. Lao-tzu personifies the spirit of early Taoism.

CHUANG-TZU

Chuang-tzu lived approximately 250 years after Lao-tzu; he was a contemporary of Mencius, in the kingdom of Wei. He worked in the city Khi-yuan, close to where Lao-tzu had lived. Chuang-tzu was a skillful writer whose satirical pen jabbed at other contemporary philosophers through stories in which Lao-tzu trumped philosophers (such as Confucius) of other systems.

King Wei of Chu heard about Chuang-tzu's ability to express profound concepts with clarity and wit. One day the king sent messengers laden with gifts to invite Chuang-tzu to court in the hope of offering him the position of prime minister. The messengers found Chuang-tzu quietly fishing. Without even turning his head, Chuang-tzu responded with a broad smile and said, "I am honored that the king would like to have me as his minister, since this is certainly a high and noble position. But I have heard that the king of Chu keeps a sacred tortoise who lived three thousand years carefully enclosed in a chest on the altar. Now I ask you, would the tortoise rather be dead and have his remains revered or be alive and splashing in the mud?"

The messengers could not help but answer, "Of course, it would rather be alive, playing in the mud."

Chuang-tzu answered, "Then leave me now. I would rather be free to splash in the mud than be subject to the rules and restrictions of the king's court!"

Chuang-tzu lived a life free of restrictions, true to his personal expression of Taoism. He taught students and wrote, holding a simple job as a minor official in the province of Men. He devoted his entire life to the Taoist Way.

THE TAO

In its unity it is called the secret.
The secret's still deeper secret
is the gateway through which all miracles emerge.
—*Tao Te Ching*, Book I, translated by Wilhelm

Taoism puts all its faith in the Tao as the source of wisdom. True wisdom of the Tao is mysterious and inexpressible in words. Paradoxically, carefully accumulating bits of data and learning from external sources to achieve wisdom leads away from the Tao, according to the early Taoists. Tao is the deeper nature in everything, everywhere. If Tao is the Way, then it follows that words and concepts cannot truly express it; it must instead be accepted and followed.

Return to the simplicity of Oneness of all things, and everything will be well. Banish the search for external, superficial knowledge, and true wisdom can grow. Do not measure or control things by external standards or techniques. Seek the measure of things within (Yu-tang 1942, 687). Then contentment, long life, health, and vitality flow.

MEDITATION

The path to the Tao is through meditation. In the *Tao Te Ching*, Lao-tzu alludes to the calm meditation that brings us to the emptiness where we can find Tao:

Attaining the utmost vacuity and earnestly observing quietness, while the ten thousand things all together are operating, I thus contemplate their return (to nothingness) (Duyvendak 1992, 49).

Chuang-tzu tells a story in which Confucius approaches Lao-tzu, who is sitting still as a stone. Lao-tzu eventually stops meditating and answers Confucius' question as to what he was doing. "I am wandering in the beginning of things." This is Taoism's way of describing meditation.

NONACTION

Nonaction is the Way in Taoism. It does not mean literally doing nothing. Action almost seems to happen by itself. Nonaction implies doing important things by letting them be rather than by making them be. This requires sensitivity to the capacity within things and events to generate spontaneously and control themselves. This idea is similar to the Western concept of actualization (explained in the next chapter). Taoists believe that noninterference with the natural way of people and events results in the flawless perfection of action. Action takes place through nonaction.

Leaders who used Taoist principles to rule were not controlling and structure-oriented. They were flexible, allowing for the uniqueness of each situation. Taoists advised governments to step out of the way, be humble, act without goals or purpose, desire nothing for themselves, to make the will of the people their own. The ruler stands back, not needing law and force to create order, instead providing calmness and bringing about peace. "He practices nonaction and consequently there is nothing that is not well governed" (Duyvendak 1992, 24).

Through nonaction, a ruler permits a moral order to emerge naturally. Domination and conquest may ultimately result in the ruler's submission and defeat, for they contain the seeds of decay and destruction. History shows that violence and anger do not end when war is over or the deed is done. Negative consequences may last far longer, leading to long-standing feuds and animosity. Taoism does not resist in this way. Instead, another solution is offered. The same principles apply to personal conduct.

YIN AND YANG

Identifying with the Tao and nonaction ultimately leads to transcendence. Acceptance of nothing leads to acceptance of something. Lao-tzu teaches people how to use opposites to achieve goals. Start from the low to reach the high. Retract first in order to expand later. The thing contains its opposite. "The Way is constantly inactive and yet there is nothing that remains undone" (Book 37, translated by Duyvendak).

Tao is the inner Way, the cosmic order. The inner Way leads the Taoists to the One, the unity of all things. The One leads to the two, called the yin-yang, the opposites, being and nonbeing, form and emptiness. The two leads to the three, often thought to be heaven, earth, and man. Form, emptiness, and synthesis of the three leads to the ten thousand things, the multiplicity of reality. Ancient yin-yang philosophy, implicit in the *Book of History* and the *Book of Changes* (*I Ching*), meshed well with Taoism. Although the Tao is unfathomable, its Oneness manifests itself in our world as the union of opposites. Thus, we know the Tao in all its differentiations into yin and yang.

Simply stated, yin-yang theory holds that everything exists by virtue of its opposite and has no meaning without its opposite. For example, we understand lightness because we have darkness. Up is always in relation to down. By recognizing that the two are in a mutual relationship as one, we can reach a more profound understanding. The apparent objects and events in our world are a function of the Tao. When the two return to the One, a more inclusive perspective emerges.

INNER SPIRIT: CHI

Taoism emphasizes sensitivity to the inner spirit; the energy of the inner spirit is known as *chi*. Chi is the breath of life, the spirit that stirs all nature to be alive. The passage that is often interpreted to refer to chi is in Book X of the *Tao Te Ching:* Can you make your breath soft like the breath of an infant? Early Taoists were vague in their references, perhaps so as not to mislead followers with "concepts." Chi is perceived externally in nature itself, more subtly in the interaction of world events, and internally within the body.

Taoist practitioners inevitably develop concepts and methods by which to communicate the spirit of the Tao through chi. Taoist artists express the flow of chi with brushstrokes. Painters use nature to symbolize the patterns of chi. Bamboo, because of its hollow core, is considered the symbolic epitome of the Tao.

Breathing exercises unblock and enhance chi for health and longevity, utilizing techniques drawn from the implications of Taoist theory. Innovations continue today in Chinese medicine. Tai chi and chi-kung are martial arts that are imbued with Taoism and raise chi through specialized movements.

The vitality of chi is an energy within all phenomena. Artists, healers, and martial artists attune themselves to it. Through sensitivity to the life force of chi, Tao inspires and gives substance, technique, and guidance.

TAOISM AND CONFUCIANISM COMPARED

> *When the great Way declines, there is "humanity"*
>   *and "justice."*
> *When cleverness and knowledge appear, there is*
>   *"great artificiality."*
> *When the six degrees of kinship do not live in*
>   *harmony, there are "filial sons."*
> *When state and dynasty are plunged in disorder,*
>   *there are "loyal ministers."*
>   —*Tao Te Ching,* Book XVIII translated by Duyvendak

Taoism differs fundamentally from Confucianism in ways that this passage addresses. The two philosophies vied for monarchs' support. Sometimes Taoism was favored, sometimes Confucianism. Eventually the two philosophies merged in their applications, drawing from the best of each.

Confucius taught how correctly appreciating ethical values in human relations brings about good and civil behavior. Lao-tzu and Chuang-tzu believed that externally imposed rules and laws take people away from the Tao, that such codes are external, superficial, and distracting. People have an intuitive sense of correctness and truth: the Tao. Therefore, efforts to articulate it or follow traditional customs, rules, or rituals lead people astray. For Taoism the natural Way is the correct Way. A structured, orderly society was unnecessary. Oneness with the Tao is a better guide.

In the same manner as Hinduism, Confucianism encourages vertical hierarchies defined by the culture and moderated by a complex network of role relationships. Taoism claims that such hierarchical structure should not dominate society, nor should any culture be forced to submit to them. Interaction should be subtle, a seamless interrelationship among lateral networks.

Although Taoists and Confucianists differ in their methods, they both seek to help people become sincere, humble, and honest. The Taoists hold that a person's development follows naturally from Oneness with the Tao. The criterion or standard of behavior should be within the Tao itself. The sincerity that Confucianists seek would then come naturally. The virtues that Confucianism hoped to develop were to the Taoists a function of the Tao in each person. "When you do not cultivate your own person, and make the cultivation of others your object, are you not occupying yourself with what is external?" (Legge 1962, 198.) Letting go of these concerns permits the Way to emerge clearly from within. Then people will become sincere, honest, and humble without effort. Letting go is the entry to the Way.

Taoism guides people to return to the source: the natural self. Taoists gain a kind of control and almost paranormal sensitivity to events by following the Tao. This philosophy is individualistic and yet paradoxically universal. The *Tao Te Ching* advises people to deal with the great while it is still small, the difficult while it is easy. To pass from the small to the great is then natural and simple: one step at a time. "The journey of a thousand miles begins with one step" (*Tao Te Ching*, Book LXIV translated by Legge).

6
WEST MEETS EAST

To us, alas, sight and sound, inner and outer, soul
and body, God and World, have fallen apart. What
we knew as children we now must grope for. Only
grown-up children—artists and wise men—know
this always, radiating life in their glance, listening
to the blossoming around.

—Erich M. v. Hornbostel, Gestalt psychologist

M ost Eastern philosophies begin with an assumption of unity.
Many Western views analyze everything into constituent
parts to be categorized. Yet, there are some Western per-
spectives that also start from unity. When integrated with Eastern philosophy, these Western theories (which combine unity with analytic
thinking) give us a greater understanding of ourselves, at One with
our universe.

GESTALT PSYCHOLOGY

The Gestalt psychologists, a group who came to America from Ger-
many in the early 1900s, believed that unity, a Gestalt as they called
it, is primary to how we perceive. They explained that it is a natural
tendency to perceive things as organized wholes. We perceive form

and constancy in our world. This Gestalt, or whole, is more primary than its constituent elements. Although some ideas of Gestalt psychology were abandoned as the years passed, this conception of patterning, organization, and unity is generally accepted by most perceptual psychologists and cognitive scientists today.

Organization and subsequent interaction influences how we experience and interpret things. Grouping affects our comprehension and, indeed, the perceived identity of the object. The Gestalt psychologists used this concept in comprehending all phenomena. For example, without the tendency to form an interacting unity among the parts, learning and memorizing becomes more difficult. We look for a commonality, to group items that belong together, in order to memorize or learn better.

GESTALT PRINCIPLES OF PERCEPTION

The Gestaltists believed that patterning and grouping of stimuli follow certain laws of perception. Things that are similar tend to get grouped together. For example, look at these series of circles:

We tend to see the large circles together and the small dots together. We group them together, automatically, without trying, when we perceive them. They can be perceived differently, but it is not as likely. Habit and past experience also determine patterns. If the letters AB are usually together and then are paired with C, then ABC tends to be perceived. With practice, we can learn to perceive more openly.

Perception organizes itself automatically. You can understand this by looking at the following figure:

M

W

M and *W*, when brought together, tend to be seen together. How close together things are (proximity) and the tendency to form a unity (gestalt) predominate in perception.

The interaction of parts is important, but the whole is not just the sum of its parts. Break a stick, and it is two sticks. Break a spear, it is not two spears. One part is the pointed part, one the shaft—but the unity is shattered.

Edgar Rubin, a Danish psychologist, studied and formulated the figure-ground theory. When we look at something, the unity we perceive includes a figure and a background. The background is intimately involved in creating the figure, and vice versa.

Look at the picture. First, look at the black object, viewed as the figure. What do you see? Now shift your focus to consider the white spaces the figure. Can you see something different? This is the phenomenon of figure-ground. You tend to see first one, then the other pattern, depending on your perspective.

INSIGHT

The addition of things together, the parts of the object, do not make an object without some unitary principle or boundary. This unity is perceived as a meaningful pattern. The parts or elements become part of the unity, almost seeming to jump out at us. Gestalt psychologists call this experience "insight." The phenomenon of insight closely parallels sudden enlightenment in Zen.

Insight derives from a clear perception of the interrelationship of the whole. Insight is not apart from or outside the situation but rather is a clear understanding of the meaning and potential character *within* the situation. Thus, it is similar to enlightenment in that nothing is added, nothing new is learned. Instead, the actual interrelationship is comprehended. The interrelationship expresses its potential for meaning.

Insight often occurs suddenly, in a flash, like sudden enlightenment. You probably noticed this when you looked at the different figures above. One figure seems to jump out as the pattern. Then, when you consider it from another perspective, the figure shifts suddenly, so that you see it differently.

Insight is part of successful problem solving. Selecting the best method to tackle a problem depends on correctly perceiving the situation. For example, imagine that a hungry monkey is locked in a cage with a stick. A banana is placed outside the cage, at nearly the stick's length away from him. At some point he suddenly recognizes that the stick can be used as a tool to get the banana: this is insight. If the monkey has never been shown how to use a stick as a tool before, past experience is probably not a factor in his insight. Instead, the monkey discovers that the stick can be used in a new way, as a tool to get the banana.

The past need not limit us. The present is new, not just based on what has been. Seek the gaps, discover what is missing in the Gestalt, the missing parts of the pattern. Thus, the empty space can also be meaningful. Open your mind to allow insight to happen, in the present moment, through meditation.

SELF-ACTUALIZATION

We can say that there is in every organism, at whatever level, an underlying flow of movement toward constructive fulfillment of its inherent possibilities (Rogers 1980, 117).

In the 1930s Kurt Goldstein examined brain-damaged soldiers. He found that their mental abilities regrouped to form unified systems to help them continue functioning as best they could. He was amazed that these people coped creatively and inventively even with diminished resources. He saw positive possibilities: people will find ways to be the best they can be, to fulfill their potential. He called this tendency self-actualization. It was the beginning of a new theory of motivation that was to form the basis for the "third force," humanistic psychology.

Psychologist Arthur Combs reinterpreted self-actualization to help normal people understand what motivates them. Human beings seek to fulfill themselves. Self-actualization is a general motivational drive that can be a powerful stimulus to achieving your life's dreams and goals. Life is forward and positive.

Life seeks completion and satisfaction, through fulfillment of its true nature. The "true man of no rank" of Zen master Lin-chi, the "gentlemen" of Confucius, the Taoist sage, and the Yogi are all counterparts of the ideal of the actualized person. They seek to become what they must be in their true inner nature. There is an inner urge compelling life to wholeness, completion. This tendency in all living beings to wholeness is parallel to the exhibited tendency to closure in Gestalt psychology, to form a unity, a whole. This tendency also motivates and urges human beings to action that fulfills their inner needs.

Actualization is a tendency for people to fulfill their potential, developing and evolving toward wholeness. In perception, in our earlier example, when we are presented with a number of stimuli, we naturally seek some pattern, some organization that is meaningful (as when perceiving the circles and dots). Then there is a release from the pattern as a new figure begins to come into being. Actualization is similar.

We are always in the process of becoming, of expressing our true nature, in relation to background. The whole person is primary, not individual personality characteristics, piecemeal aspects of functioning. When we focus on the whole, things work out and difficulties can be resolved.

Expectations about the limits of these possibilities, quite naturally, become taken for granted, a perceived world of experience. A major part of change, then, is to change the map of expectancies of what we believe is possible, to accept that another way is possible. Expected actions tend to be the ones we pursue. We map out our destiny from what we imagine is possible. Meditation can take us back to the territory itself, opening the possibilities for alternative pathways.

The Way may be followed through the outer form or through seeking the inner form, in actions that seem formal or ones that seem informal, through spontaneous expression or expressions that are highly structured and formalized. The Way is actually none of these; it is not identical with or limited to form. Form can express the Way, yet it cannot contain or freeze it for long. As water can change its form to suit its container, yet never change its nature, so, too, with the Way.

Each Way described in the various Eastern philosophies has its own form and beliefs. These differences have resulted in various institutions that disseminate the teachings and offer people roles. Yet, these philosophies share a common thread: the inner person.

All that we do and are in life begins with the inner person. Only from the basis of a calm and aware mind can we hope to realize our potential in the world around us. These philosophies guide us to live a happy and fulfilled life, a good life, a hopeful life, always from the starting point of the inner mind of the individual. Nothing need interfere with finding fulfillment if we are aware and live in accord with our innermost true nature.

PART TWO

Clearing the Way

We do not determine what we will think, we only open
our senses, clear away as we can all obstructions from
the fact, and suffer the intellect to see.
—Ralph Waldo Emerson

All forms of meditation require mental skills such as concentration of
attention, visualization, and body awareness. Some forms of meditation apply these skills consciously and deliberately; others unconsciously
and intuitively. Different people have different needs and capacities. Some
find a narrowly focused attention to detail helpful; others benefit more
from relaxing their inhibitions, to widen their attention to the whole.
Experiment to find what works best for you, to broaden your skills or
build upon the skills you already have.

Tools that make it easier to meditate are presented here in Part II.
These exercises give you an opportunity to hone your mental tools:
sharpening concentration, directing your attention to inner and outer
experiences, and developing body awareness.

Part II also guides you in techniques of meditation, drawn from the
traditions of Yoga, Buddhism, Zen, Taoism, and Confucianism. Western traditions provide further techniques. When the customary flow of thinking

is cleared away, you may discover inner resources and capacities that you did not know you had. Experiment with classic exercises along with modern adaptations that may speak to you more directly.

7
MENTAL
TOOLS

When the waves are choppy,
it is difficult for the moon to appear.

—Chinul, Korean Zen master

Y oga has developed mental concentration into a highly evolved discipline. As Patañjali said, "Yoga is restraining the mind-stuff from taking various forms" (Yutang 1942, 120). Zen considers attention primary and trains it through meditative exercises. Western cognitive psychology accords attention prime importance in learning, memory, and all intellectual functioning. William James, the founder of American Psychology, thought that focus comes from the mind through the use of attention.

Attention is the taking possession by the mind in clear and vivid form, of one out of what seem several simultaneously possible objects or trains of thought. Focalization, concentration of consciousness are of its essence (James 1896, 403–04).

We can accomplish many things in life through concentrated attention. The Yoga teacher Ramacharaka believed that focused attention is connected with genius. "The best definition of genius is the power of concentrating upon some one given subject until its possibilities are exhausted and absorbed" (Ramacharaka, 1934 107).

Concentration takes place naturally and spontaneously when you are interested and involved in something. Carefully sensing objects around you and your inner experience of them can develop your focused presence. The following series of exercises combines the sensory-awareness training of Charlotte Selver and Charles Brooks with Yoga concentration.

OUTER FOCUSED ATTENTION

Bring a small stone that interests you to your meditation place. The stone could be rough or smooth, brightly colored or dull, anything you find visually interesting. Set it down in front of you and sit down. Look at the stone for several minutes. Notice everything you can about it: its shape, color, texture, size, how the light affects it, and anything else that you see. Keep your attention on the stone. If your mind wanders to something else, bring it back.

Focus of concentration is not limited to visual perception. You can also use your other senses, like your sense of touch, to help you develop concentration skills. In the next exercise you can experiment with focusing your attention on touch.

USING TOUCH FOR OUTER FOCUS EXERCISE

Lie on your back and relax. Place the stone on your stomach and close your eyes. Focus all your attention on the sensation of the stone resting on your stomach. Can you feel how heavy it is? Is it warmer or cooler than your skin? Can you feel the texture of the stone? Keep your attention focused on your sensations. Move the stone around, to your arm or leg, and repeat the exercise.

One doorway to higher consciousness is through control of thought. The skills developed in the outer concentration exercise also help you focus inward. The following exercise helps you unite the inner and outer worlds of experience.

INNER CONCENTRATION EXERCISE

Do this exercise immediately after the previous one. Sit comfortably and close your eyes. Recall the stone. Think about what you noticed when the stone was resting on your stomach. For some the recollection will be vivid, for others it might be vague. What is most important is that you concentrate on the recalled experience. Keep focused for at least several minutes. If you find your mind wandering, bring your attention back to the imagined experience .

VISUALIZATION EXERCISE

Sit comfortably on the floor. Look closely at your stone for several minutes. Then close your eyes. Relax your body for a moment. Visualize the stone. Keep your mind focused only on the stone. Think of nothing else. If you have difficulty doing so, open your eyes, look at the stone, relax for a moment, and then close your eyes again.

Work with this series of exercises over several days until you can remain focused for longer periods of time, up to ten minutes. You can vary all the exercises by using different stones.

8
BODY TOOLS

During speech, silence, action, and stillness, the
essence is at peace.

—Chinul, Korean Zen master

T he practice of meditation teaches you how to unify your mind with your body. Mental tools, like the ones in Chapter 7, teach you how to concentrate and visualize using your mental faculties. Body awareness can also be a focus for meditation. By performing certain movements with full awareness, mental skills develop automatically.

Dogen believed that zazen would unify the mind with the body. Both mind and body contribute equally when learning meditation. One of his disciples asked him if the Way was attained through the mind or through the body. He answered as follows:

In Zen the Way is attained with both body and mind. . . . Those who gained enlightenment by seeing blossoms or hearing sounds achieved it through the body. Therefore, if you cast aside completely the thoughts and concepts of the mind and concentrate on zazen alone, you attain to an intimacy with the Way. The attainment of the Way is truly accomplished with the body. For this reason, I urge you to concentrate on zazen (Masunaga 1971, 47).

You can develop mental clarity directly or indirectly, through awareness of your body sensations. The following exercises will help you reduce distractions by focusing your attention on your body sensations.

DELIBERATE RELAXATION EXERCISE

You can become more relaxed by focusing your attention on muscle tension and learning to let go.

Lie down on your back on the floor or outdoors on the grass. Let your arms rest on the floor beside you, with your legs slightly apart. Close your eyes. Focus your attention on your muscles. Beginning at your head, scan through your body. Do you notice any tight muscles? When a muscle is tight, there is a corresponding sensation that you can learn to recognize. If you are not sure how to recognize it, gently touch the area that you think is tight with the palm of your hand. The muscle will be slightly taut. Find the corresponding sensation of tightness.

Tension is characteristically carried in certain areas of the body, such as the shoulders, neck, or back. Compare the sensations in your neck muscles with those in your arms. Do you notice a difference? When you find an area that feels tight, concentrate all your attention there and try to relax those muscles. When you relax, there is a feeling of letting go, of opening up, a dropping away of tension. Continue to scan through your body, relaxing as you go.

If you cannot relax, ask yourself if something is wrong. Do you have a strained muscle? Or does the tension signify that there is something you should contemplate? If so, thoughts about it will usually occur to you. Later exercises address this matter. For now, simply notice and remember for later work.

DIFFERENTIAL RELAXATION EXERCISE

Lie down on your back on the floor, with your legs and arms extended outward. Close your eyes. Try to relax as much as possible. Raise your left arm straight up toward the ceiling. Form a tight fist as you allow your entire arm to become tight. Meanwhile, keep all your other muscles relaxed. You may find that your right arm automatically tightens up, too, but try to relax it even though the left arm is tensed. Hold this position for about thirty seconds, then lower your left arm and relax all your muscles. Repeat the process, only with your right arm. Then try it with your legs. Raise one leg and flex your foot while you keep your other leg relaxed. Follow the instructions used with your arms. Relax deeply all over. Do you feel calm now, in mind and body?

INDIRECT BODY RELAXATION EXERCISE

Taoism encourages us to let things be, to allow what is. In this exercise you can allow relaxation to occur naturally, as is the Taoist Way.

Lie down on your back. Raise your knees, with your feet resting flat on the floor. This position will allow your back to flatten out a bit. Close your eyes. Breathe comfortably. Pay attention to the sensations of your body, noticing where you are tight and where you are relaxed. Do not do anything other than be very attentive to your physical sensations. Continue to breathe gently. Do your tensions begin to ease of themselves? As you stay with what is, your body will find its own natural level of relaxation.

VISUALIZING RELAXATION EXERCISE

Visual imagery is a pathway for meditation. When you visualize yourself being relaxed, your body responds. Your body is not separate from your mind.

Sit or lie down. Allow yourself to be comfortable. Close your eyes. Imagine that your body is becoming very relaxed. Recall a time when you felt that way—perhaps when you were enjoying the company of good friends, maybe when you were on vacation or out in nature. Picture yourself in the situation. Some will have a vivid memory; others might have a vague picture. Fill in sensory details. Do you recall your feelings? Can you remember the sounds? Were there any distinctive smells? As you meditate on this image, does your body begin to relax of itself? Allow this to happen. Pay attention to how relaxation feels.

RELAXING THROUGH THE DAY EXERCISE

Sometimes people tense up more than they need to. A certain amount of tension is healthy, to mobilize the body for challenges; but unnecessary tension can waste energy, exhausting your resources. It is possible to notice when you are radiating extra tension, and then to let go of it by learning to occasionally glance inward during activity.

Have you ever noticed yourself tightening up as you wait in line at the store or when you are sitting at your desk? These can be opportunities for an inward glance—a meditative moment. You can do it so subtly that no one else need notice that you are turning your attention inward, studying what you feel. Notice your body sensations. Is your jaw clenched? Are your shoulders raised? Is your back hunched? Is your stomach tight or hurting? Do your legs and arms feel tight? When you are tense, ask yourself whether you need such tension. Are you reacting to something, or is the tension unnecessary? Try to relax gently those spots where you notice tension that you do not need. You will find times when you can allow yourself to be more relaxed in your daily life.

BREATHING MEDITATION SERIES

Yoga, Taoism, Buddhism, and Zen all use breathing as a focal point for attention. Breathing involves more than just inhaling and exhaling. Breathing is the source of energy in ourselves, intimately associated with our feelings and thoughts. We breathe differently when we are excited or afraid than when we are calm. Our breathing is also linked to our thoughts. You can use your own breathing to become aware and focused.

ATTENTION TO BREATHING I

This introductory breathing exercise helps you concentrate on your breathing at will for a fixed period of time. Sit comfortably, with your back relatively straight so that your breathing passages are clear. Close your eyes. Count each breath as it goes in and then out. Count to ten and then begin again. Do not alter your breathing in any way. Simply count. Do not let your attention wander. If it does, bring it back as soon as you can. Stay with your breathing for several minutes. What happens? Pay attention to what you experience. If a thought or feeling distracts you, follow the thought for a while, then return to your counting as soon as you can. Note what the thought or feeling is about.

ATTENTION TO BREATHING II

Sit quietly, with your legs crossed and your back relatively straight. Let your hands rest comfortably in your lap. Close your eyes. Focus your attention on the sensation of breathing. Feel the air going in through your nose and down into your lungs, then traveling out through your nose again. For this exercise, do not count your breaths. Instead, notice only your feelings and sensations. Do not alter anything. Do not force your breaths to be deeper or more shallow. Simply follow the passage of air in and out of your lungs using all of your awareness. Stay with your breathing for five minutes (or longer, with practice). What do you observe? How do you feel?

ATTENTION TO BREATHING III

Some time when you are feeling something intensely—perhaps while watching a scene from a movie or a play or listening to music, or perhaps while with a person to whom you react strongly—try paying attention to your breathing. What is it like? Do you spontaneously breathe deeper or shallower than before? Do you hold your breath? Observe carefully. Take a moment to notice your breathing during your various emotive reactions to people, situations, and events throughout your day.

As a variation, pay attention to other people's breathing. Are they holding their breath, breathing shallowly or deeply?

9

USING THE TOOLS TO
CLEAR YOUR MIND

*There is nothing to be grasped. We simply teach you
how to understand your original mind.*
— Huang-po, Zen master (d. 850)

All the mental skills that you have been working on in the
previous chapters can be applied to meditation. This chapter will guide you in using the tools of attention, concentration, visualization, and body awareness to meditate.

One of the most fundamental meditative abilities is clearing the
mind. Thinking has an important place in life, as it always has and always will. But excessive thinking can interfere with mental functioning. When you take some time to clear away excess thought, you
experience a pleasant calmness and a clarity of perspective. The meditations in this group will teach you how to clear your mind.

FIRST STEPS TO CLEARING THE MIND EXERCISE

With all the mental chattering from inconsequential thoughts, many people find it difficult to simply stop thinking. We often experience things most vividly when there is contrast. This exercise can get you started by giving you an automatic reaction of calm through contrast.

Turn on the television to an annoying channel. Turn up the volume. Close your eyes and listen. Permit your reaction. You may substitute another experience of the same sort, for example, listening to a radio station that plays music you do not like. After several minutes have passed, get up and turn off the television. Notice the immediate contrast of silence and relief. Allow this experience to spread, as your mind becomes calm and clear.

CLEARING THE MIND MEDITATION SERIES

Find a place where you will be uninterrupted. The exact time, place, and clothing are not important as long as you are comfortable and will not be distracted by them. Sit in the posture you find most comfortable. Close your eyes and relax your breathing.

MEDITATION I

Imagine a vast blankness. Some people like to picture a blackboard covered with scribbles, which they then erase. This blankness could be white or black, perhaps an infinite sky. Use any image that symbolizes nothingness to you. Think about this image and only this image. Picture it as vividly as you can. Sustain it for one minute if you are new to meditation, gradually working your way up to ten minutes by adding a minute at a time as you are able. Be sensitive to your own timing. Some people like to meditate for a longer time; others benefit greatly from as little as a few minutes a day. Find your own rhythm.

CLASSIC ZAZEN FOR CLEARING THE MIND

Zen Buddhists have practiced a form of clearing-the-mind meditation for centuries. Japanese Zen master Dogen believed that *zazen,* as he called this meditative exercise, was the best way to find enlightenment.

Below are the classical instructions for zazen that have been given for centuries. Today this form of meditation continues to be a well-traveled path for calm and insight.

ZAZEN: MEDITATION II

Zazen is best performed in a quiet room that is not too hot or too cold nor too light or too dark. You should not have eaten or drunk much beforehand. You should wear loose but neat clothing.

Set a thick pillow on the floor and then add a second, smaller one on top. Sit down on the pillows and cross your legs. Let your hands rest in your lap, with your thumbs touching in the center. Keep your body straight, without leaning to one side or the other. Your mouth should be gently closed, and your eyes may be open slightly. Let your breathing become calm and steady. Do not focus your gaze on anything in particular.

Begin by simply sitting and not thinking about anything in particular. If a thought or wish arises, bring it to your consciousness; notice the wish or thought as it is. Do not evaluate it. Simply observe that it is. Then allow it to leave. In doing this, you will gradually become aware of both your thinking and your not thinking. Eventually you will find a no-mindedness that is neither thinking nor not thinking.

Dogen wrote, "If you practice in this way for a long time, you will forget all attachments and concentration will come naturally. That is the art of zazen" (Dumoulin 1990, 76).

TAOIST MIND-CLEARING: MEDITATION III

Taoists also have meditative methods for clearing the mind. Sit comfortably and relax your body. Close your eyes. Let your thoughts drift, without thinking about anything in particular. You do not need to do anything. Simply sit quietly, allowing yourself to be just as you are. Let your breathing become comfortable and your body continue to relax itself. Spend at least ten minutes doing this.

VISUALIZATION MIND-CLEARING: MEDITATION IV

In this exercise you will use visualization to help give you an experience of calm, clear mind. Lie down on your back, with your knees up and your feet flat on the floor. Let your arms rest by your side, palms up. Close your eyes. Picture a vista of grassy hills, rolling as far as you can see. The clear blue sky meets the green hillside. All is quiet, still. In fact, it is so quiet that you can almost hear your own heartbeat. Your muscles will relax a bit, effortlessly. The colors are soothing; the breeze is soft. As you look at this peaceful scene, your thoughts slow down—leaving an experience of calm and stillness. Do not do anything other than enjoy the scene.

Meditative calmness, once experienced and made your own, can be practiced anytime, anywhere. Consider any situation an opportunity to practice, to extend calmness deliberately throughout your life.

PART THREE

On the Way

Calm, activity—each has its use.

Zen Master Shaku Soen (1859-1919)

Upon achieving inner tranquillity, the meditator discovers a certain balance point, poised in the middle, cup empty, ready to fulfill his or her destiny in wholehearted action. Although people sometimes think of meditation as simply quieting the mind, meditation can be an active process, intimately involved with living your life.

Meditation helps us focus on action. Sometimes we do things first and think about them after. Other times we think things through carefully, then we act. Thought leads to action, and action leads back to thought. But thought is not just a function of action alone. Our feelings are an insepara-ble part of action, too: we feel emotions about what we do and about what others do. We cannot exclude feelings. Our feelings change as our actions and those of others change. Therefore, we can affect our feelings by changing our actions. The same logic applies to thoughts. Thoughts are linked to action: we tend to think differently when we act differently. When our thoughts change, our actions and feelings change. Through the use of meditation, you can bring your attention to what you think and feel as you do things. Any part of the interaction can effect change.

Part III brings meditation into the realm of action, to help you overcome obstacles and follow through with your life's commitments. You can meditate just before, during, or directly after doing something. Keep in mind that all meditation, whether done quietly or actively, not doing or doing, is always an inner experience.

The dictionary has numerous definitions for action: the process of acting or doing, to behave and conduct oneself, to render, to carry out, to produce, to effect, to attend to, to give, to have as an occupation, to move, to travel, to meet the needs of, and so on. An act is the deed accomplished by means of an action. Whether the action is purposeful and deliberate or spontaneous and unplanned, meditation can enhance the process of acting and doing. Therefore, when we talk about meditation in action, we refer to most of what we are involved in throughout life.

The calm, clear awareness that you develop by meditating can prepare you for action and even take you through it. Zen Buddhists believe that all of life's experiences offer an opportunity to practice meditation. Walking, sitting, eating, sleeping—all are opportunities to meditate. The following chapters show many ways to develop and maintain meditative awareness as you engage in the activities of your daily life.

8
THE BEGINNING PATH

We act, and the fruits
Of our actions
Ripen, to
Become to be
Borne on winds of destiny.

—C. Alexander Simpkins

EMPTYING THE MIND FOR ACTION

Many of the Eastern philosophies believe that when you discover emptiness in meditation, obstructions fall away and everything becomes possible. The swordsmen of feudal Japan used Zen meditation in their quest to become invincible in battle. The lessons that meditation held for them were not limited to technique alone. They learned to use their mind in a particular way—clearing away distractions to reach a state of no-mindedness. Then their body could perform automatically, doing what they had trained for without any interference from thoughts or feelings.

Even the most ferocious samurai would take time out just before entering into battle, to prepare by sitting quietly in meditation, drinking tea. It was believed that the state of mind brought about by the tea ceremony was more important than all the sword techniques put together. The following Zen story illustrates this point.

Once there was a man who had mastered the Zen art of tea. Through a simple tea ceremony, he could give his guests a taste of the Zen state of no-mind. He was retained by a noble samurai to conduct tea ceremonies. Together, they would become absolutely calm and attuned to the moment. One day the samurai was called to the city on business. He asked the tea master to accompany him. The master was reluctant, because the city was a very unsafe place, with roving bandits and out-of-work swordsmen looking for a fight. The samurai suggested that the tea master could dress as a samurai and borrow one of his swords. Then, he assured him, no one would bother him. The tea master agreed.

While the samurai was attending to his business, his companion decided to take a walk through the city streets. Unthinkingly, the tea master bumped into a large, rough-looking swordsman, who misinterpreted the action. He said gruffly, "You have offended me. We must fight!"

The tea master tried to dissuade him, but the swordsman insisted. Realizing that there was no way out of the situation, the tea master agreed to fight with him the next morning. The tea master was worried. Later that evening, he told his friend about the encounter, and said in a shaky voice, "What shall I do? I know nothing about fighting and I am certain to die!"

The samurai replied, "Let us have tea."

The two of them sat down together. The tea master began to perform the ritual, and a tranquil, peaceful state of mind came over him. He seemed like a man without a care in the world.

"Approach your opponent with the mind of tea," advised the samurai. "Then raise your sword over your head and run toward him." The tea master agreed.

The next morning the burly swordsman was waiting. But the opponent he encountered seemed to be a different man. The tea master stood tall. With absolute confidence, he raised his sword determined that both would die, and began walking boldly toward the swordsman. Faced with this, the swordsman stepped back and said, "I see that you are ready to die. You show me honor. I release you." He bowed his head, placed his sword back in its holder, and ran away. The tea master faced the life-and-death encounter with the help of the calm mind of tea. The swordsman recognized his spirit, and chose, wisey, to back down.

It was the teamaster's state of mind, not his technique, that made the difference. Set yourself properly, and your action will flow naturally. Meditating on a ritual like the tea ceremony can help you set the stage for action by freeing yourself from limitations.

TEA CEREMONY TO EMPTY YOUR MIND

The ritual of tea may be used now, as it has been used for more than a thousand years, to clear away distractions and ready you for action. It is a way to return to a simple, direct process of experiencing. Zen tea masters have performed tea ceremonies for centuries to help people become attuned to themselves and their situation.

The decor of the tea room is simple. A single plant placed in an earthenware vase and a small calligraphic scroll hung on the wall are the only decoration. A fiber mat covers the floor near a small hearth. A tea kettle is set over a small fire. A small group of people are seated on the mat, quietly enjoying the meditative experience. For a short while, the tea ceremony takes them away from the stress of everyday life and back to the fundamentals of human existence: people in harmony, appreciating simple pleasures in the moment.

You might not have the luxury of a separate teahouse, or even a tea room, but the spirit of tea can be created anywhere with the appropriate atmosphere, correct attitude, and a few simple utensils. We have performed tea rituals with many people, even children and people who did not speak our language. You can perform a simple ceremony to set yourself for action.

A SIMPLE TEA CEREMONY

To create your own tea ritual, pick a comfortable place in attractive yet simple surroundings—outdoors in a quiet park or perhaps in your own backyard. You could prepare a special corner in your house. Bring in one or two things to look at, such as a simple plant or a single flower in a plain vase. An uncomplicated picture may add to the atmosphere.

The utensils should also be simple: a small teapot, Oriental-style teacups (no handles), tea leaves or herbal tea chopped and placed in a small bowl, a spoon, and a kettle of hot water. We like to use peppermint tea because of its minty aroma and taste, but any tea will do. Some people also use a whisk to stir powdered tea. One person is the host who performs the ceremony. The guests are instructed on the procedures when they sit down together. Participants are encouraged to listen to the sounds, smell the aroma of the tea, taste the delicate flavor. All is to be savored.

The ceremony begins. The host invites all the guests to share a brief meditation. After a few minutes, when it feels like it is time to begin, the participants quietly turn their full attention to the host, who makes the tea and pours it. After receiving their tea, the guests and host drink their tea together. No words need to be spoken throughout the ceremony. Everyone notices many details as they enjoy sharing the calming experience of tea.

There are formal tea traditions that can be practiced as well. People train under a master, experience enlightenment, and become ordained as tea masters themselves. Tea masters can perform historically formalized rituals, such as the Japanese tea ceremony known as *cha-no-yu*. Your tea ceremony should feel comfortable, so you can dissolve the barriers between yourself and others in the moment. With the renewing experience of inner calm, you can move on to the tasks and responsibilities of your life with renewed vitality.

FILLING THE MIND FOR ACTION

When traveling, we invariably spend many hours getting ready—packing, arranging for tickets, and checking last-minute details. Motivation flows naturally when you are planning a fun vacation. But some tasks are not as easy to accomplish. Obstructions seem to crop up, making it difficult to get started. Writer's block, plateaus in athletic training, or fear of learning new things are all examples of impediments to action.

Artists, writers, and athletes often have an individualized set of rituals to ready themselves. These preparations fill the mind, paving the way for action to follow. The calligrapher prepares brushes in a repetitive pattern, getting ready for the creative act to take place. Athletes often go through a ritualized routine to prepare themselves both physically and mentally.

A deliberate personal ritual can put you in the correct mood for your task, whatever it might be. However, all meditative traditions caution against mistaking the ritual for the experience; it is only a boat in which to cross the river. Do not remain in the boat afterward, admiring it . . . continue on your journey.

READYING FOR ACTIVITY

Next time you are about to undertake a certain activity, take a few moments to prepare yourself by meditating. Create an atmosphere that makes you feel most comfortable with the activity. For example, you might like to surround yourself with your favorite books. You may find that looking at paintings on the wall helps or that playing certain music puts you in a creative mood. Some artists like certain smells, such as pipe tobacco or a stick of incense. The details are personal, which must be respected, but note what you require for your individual atmosphere. Set your tools out carefully, perhaps placing them in a certain order or in a particular way. As you do so, close your eyes and feel the weight of each one before you put it down. This may also be adapted and applied to a sport. Then move on to the next exercise.

GETTING READY WITH MEDITATION

Just before you plunge into an intense, focused activity, set yourself with meditation. Sit quietly. Visualize yourself doing the activity smoothly, as you would like to. Fill your mind entirely with this experience and nothing else. Then just sit and let your thoughts drift away while you await the correct moment to begin. The few minutes spent meditating will help you engage in the action wholeheartedly.

11
THE BASICS
OF ACTION

When you do something, if you fix your mind on the ac-
tivity with some confidence, the quality of your state of
mind is the activity itself.

—D. T. Suzuki

P eople often go through their lives with very little self-awareness. When your mind is not focused on what you are
doing, you may have difficulty recalling the action later.
Looking back on your day, you may notice that there are gaps in your
recollection. Unity of mind and body throughout the day can make a
difference on many levels, helping you to be more at ease and natural.
You become more proficient and skilled in your actions, which take
on a newly added spiritual dimension. To be one with what you are
doing is to live an enlightened life.

You can get in touch with the basic physical activities of life: lying
down, sitting, standing, and walking—the "four dignities of man"
(Brooks 1982, 21). In so doing, you become generally more aware.
Everyone engages in these activities throughout the day, every day.
But how often do you pay attention to what you are experiencing as

you lie in bed, sit at the table, stand in line, or walk down the street, unless it is a problem? If your foot hurts, you naturally become aware of every painful step. The instinct for awareness is the potential that lies within, always ready in reserve when needed. The following exercises, drawn from the sensory awareness training of Charlotte Selver and Charles Brooks, bring heightened awareness into everyday life. Do them at home or in a quiet, undisturbed place.

EXERCISE IN REPOSING

Have you ever considered lying down an activity? You can enhance your general awareness by paying very close attention to your body even when you are at rest. Lie down on your back on a padded floor or a comfortable rug (or a flat grassy area outdoors in a park or even the beach). Draw your knees up so that your feet rest flat on the floor. Place your arms by your side, palms up. Notice how this position allows your back to lie flat against the floor. Straighten out your legs again; notice the difference in your back. Return your knees to the bent position, with your feet flat. Close your eyes.

Feel how your body meets the floor. Are you sinking into the floor, or are you pressing down, holding yourself away from it? Are your muscles tight, or do they feel relaxed? Is your breathing regular and calm, or labored and tight? Are your breaths shallow or deep? Pay attention to the sensations of your body. Notice as many details as possible. Try not to think about them or conceptualize; instead, feel and sense these things from inside yourself. Refrain from judging your experience as good or bad. Do not try to put what you are feeling into words. Simply observe the feeling, and let it be, without interfering. Experience lying quietly with this heightened awareness for five or more minutes, up to twenty minutes or so. When you feel ready, gently stretch your legs and arms and sit up.

SITTING

Sitting is a fundamental position throughout life. Most of us spend many hours of our day in a seated position. You can learn to be more aware of yourself when sitting, facilitating a more efficient and comfortable body functioning. Because sitting is so central, several different seating exercises are presented.

SITTING EXERCISE: THE FLOOR

Sit cross-legged on the floor. If you cannot sit comfortably cross-legged, sit with your legs slightly apart, knees bent, with your arms around your knees. Close your eyes. Hold your head upright so that your back is fairly straight. Do not strain to be straight but do not slouch, either. You should feel a free-flow of air as you breathe gently, in and out. Allow your rib cage to move as you breathe. Pay attention to your body sensations. Do you feel comfortable, or are you fighting to keep upright? Does your breathing feel constricted? Can you let go of effort, or do you need to tense a little? Try stretching your midsection slightly. Does this open the air passages? If so, perhaps you have been slumping forward without realizing it. Be comfortable. Accepting your posture is part of body awareness, to let it be.

Experiment with your balance. Shift your position slightly several times forward and back, noticing how your muscles tighten as you move farther away from the center. Experiment with this until you begin to discover the point in the middle, aligned with gravity, where you feel at ease. Repeat this shifting with gentle side-to-side swaying. Shift from side to side until you find the relaxed center. Stay poised at the center point. Do you feel more comfortable sitting now? Breathe gently. Try to let go of unnecessary tensions again. Sometimes, after a while, you will be able to. Other times you won't be able to, and some tension may seem appropriate. Even though you feel tension, becoming aware of it and accepting it may help.

CHAIR SITTING EXERCISE

Much of our daily sitting is done in chairs, where we are not so much sitting in chairs as we are leaning on them. This exercise will help you get support from a chair while continuing to be self-supportive at the same time.

Use a desk or dining chair. Stand with your back facing the chair. Pay attention as you slowly lower yourself into the chair. Do you feel as though you are dropping into the chair, or does your body lower gracefully? Can you continue to remain balanced as you descend? Do you use your arms for support and contact? Once in the chair, how do you sit? Do you lean against the chair back? Does your back sag or are you more comfortable fairly upright? Do your feet rest on the floor, or are your feet pushing against it? Does the chair hold you, or are you holding yourself in the chair? Notice your breathing. Can you be attentive while continuing to breathe, or do you hold your breath to concentrate? How do you feel at this moment? Do you feel at ease or constrained? Consider these nuances—sense them.

Practice several times by standing up and sitting down slowly, with awareness.

STANDING

Standing upright is one important fact that distinguishes us from the animals. "To stand on your own two feet" is an expression that symbolizes independence and competence. But have you ever experienced standing without symbolism, as an activity complete in itself?

STANDING EXERCISE

Take off your shoes. Move your feet around, scrunch up your toes, tap the soles of your feet lightly. Then stand up, with your feet placed shoulder-width apart, eyes closed, and arms hanging loosely at your sides. Breathe naturally and comfortably. Notice how your feet meet the floor. Notice how wide your shoulders feel, how far it is from your feet to the top of your head. Pay attention to your skin. Does it feel warm or cool? Is there any tingling? Notice if you are tightening your muscles. Can you let go of unnecessary tension that is not involved in keeping your body upright? For example, if you notice uncomfortable tension in your shoulders, can you relax them a bit?

Experiment with your balance as you did in the floor-sitting exercise. Gently rock forward and back several times to discover your center point. Do the same thing with side-to-side swaying. Keep you feet in place. You will feel a slight discomfort, especially in your legs, when you are out of line with gravity. In time, you will discover your own best alignment with gravity, in which standing is most effortless. Allow yourself to stand for several minutes, being aware of your body posture as you do so.

WALKING

Even though we may drive or be driven places in automobiles, trains, planes, or busses, most of us spend some time each day walking. But walking need not always be for a purpose. Walking can be just an activity to enjoy, for its own sake.

WALKING EXERCISE

Take off your shoes. Stand for a moment, as you did in the previous exercise, relaxed and aligned with gravity. Very slowly take a step forward. Feel your heel as it meets the floor, then feel the ball of your foot as you roll forward. Note how your balance shifts as you step. Let your arms swing naturally. Take another slow step, paying careful attention to your sensations. Notice how you feel as you walk. Are your steps heavy, labored, or difficult? Or do you feel like a German shepherd on a leash and would rather be running? Perhaps your experience is somewhere in between. Continue to walk, paying close attention to your sensations of motion, breathing comfortably and with relaxed steps. Try different paces, slower or faster, without losing awareness. Meditate as you move.

REPOSING, SITTING, STANDING, WALKING: ADVANCED EXERCISE

Now try each of the actions in this chapter without engaging your conscious mind. If you decide to go for a walk, walk without deliberate effort, letting your steps take you where they will, with no purpose in mind. Just let walking take place. For example, take a walk in the country or on the beach—aimless, relaxed—permitting spontaneous movement for a while. Just walk. Or just stand, sit, or lie down, letting yourself experience the activity with nothing particular in mind.

All the activities that you have experienced—lying, sitting, standing, and walking—are part of everyday life. Take a moment, here and there in the day, to turn your attention to these actions, as you did in the exercises. Sometimes you may have time for only a brief inward glance. Other times perhaps you can spend several minutes sensing. In time, your habitual awareness will alter, as you consciously attend to the fundamental activities of living.

FOCUS ON MOVEMENT EXERCISE

Now that you have experimented with awareness of yourself in action, you can extend this skill to other activities. Begin this exercise by thinking about an activity that you do regularly. It could be running, swimming, or even a more mundane task like sweeping, dusting, or taking out the trash. Close your eyes. Relax your muscles wherever they may be unnecessarily contracted, and let the rhythm of breathing be natural, instinctive. Imagine performing the movement. Do not physically move very much. Imagine that you are able to perform the activity with appropriate intensity, focus, precision, balance, and speed, without excess tension. Feel the motions as you

Focus on Movement Exercise, continued

visualize them. Try to refine your performance. When you have finished, open your eyes. Now, if you can, execute the movement, in the best way possible, with your attention fully focused on what you are doing. You may need to do the second part of this exercise later. Do you perform with greater precision?

ATTENTION TO THE PRESENT EXERCISE

Pick a small number of errands that you need to do, such as trips to the bank, the gas station, and the grocery store. Before you begin, sit quietly and close your eyes. Allow your mind to clear, as in the earlier exercises. As you perform each errand, focus your attention on it as fully as you can. If you find yourself anticipating the next errand, perhaps thinking about going to the gas station as you stand in line at the bank, bring yourself back to the present moment. Concentrate on your standing. Look around at your surroundings as well as looking within your own thoughts. Observe others, not just yourself. Pay careful attention to what you feel and do, and what others do and seem to feel, too. This may lead to pleasant conversation rather than discomfort. Remain appropriately relaxed— that is, do not tense up unnecessarily. How do you feel upon completing what you set out to do? Do you appreciate those others who helped make it possible? Often we forget to take the time to feel personal satisfaction in what we have accomplished or be grateful for what others do for us.

12
ACTIVE HEALTH

We weave the cloth
Of our every day
By what we do and give
The fabric of our destiny
Is made of how we live

—C. Alexander Simpkins

I n the West, we think of medicine as a way of curing illness and disease. We go to the doctor when we are sick, unhealthy. We have not ever agreed on what *health* is, exactly. Is health the absence of illness, or is there a kind of optimum, individual healthy state? There are numerous classifications and categories of illness and diseases (not all of them even universally agreed upon), but there are not any accepted classifications of health. This is unfortunate because health is not just relief from sickness or an absence of negative symptoms: something positive is also involved. We feel well, fit, energetic. We experience our personal health as real, although sometimes we may be tricked into an incorrect judgment by the absence of symptoms. People do not always know when they are sick, but they have a definite feeling of good health when they are optimally healthy. Health and a healthy feeling are a matter of the mind and the spirit along with the body.

HEALTHY MIND

Numerous studies have shown that symptoms of physical illness correlate with mental and emotional symptoms (Wolff, 1953). This research led to the use of stress scales to anticipate and predict physical illness. Jerome D. Frank, M.D. Ph.D., a highly respected researcher at the Johns Hopkins University Medical School, pointed out a link between depression and hopelessness. Health is promoted when people feel hopeful about the future and self-confident. In the University's Psychotherapy Research Project, Frank measured feelings of hopelessness and helplessness to determine patients' health. Having faith and hope, he believed, leads to healthier living (Frank 1978, 172).

Chinese Zen master Lin-chi believed that what truly holds people back is a lack of faith in themselves.

When students today fail to make progress, where is the fault? The fault lies in the fact that they don't have faith in themselves. If you don't have faith in yourself, then you'll be forever in a hurry trying to keep up with everything around you. You'll be twisted and turned by whatever environment you're in and you can never move freely (Watson 1993, 21).

Faith and hope come from within. They affect everything you do in a positive way. Life's challenges can be met and handled well as a matter of course. Lin-chi believed that nothing special is missing. You must tap your inner resources. "Then whatever circumstances surround you, they can never pull you awry" (Watson 1993, 31). Developing the inner person, through meditation, is the key.

LIN-CHI MEDITATION

Change the direction of your thoughts from outwardly focused to inwardly focused; turn your attention inward. When with another person, "shine your light on them," as Lin-chi said (Watson, 1993, 41). Do not lose yourself in the other person's opinions about you or your situation. Rather, be aware of what you perceive. Return to this awareness deliberately from time to time during the day. Let your inner light illuminate the world for you.

NEW OPTIONS EXERCISE

When you try something you have always wanted to do, you enhance your faith in yourself and gain a hopeful feeling about life. Think about your interests and talents. Is there something that you are interested in but have never tried? Perhaps you have always wanted to paint or have wished you could play a musical instrument, or wanted to try a new sport. Whatever it is, make it manageable. Remember, you do not have to be Mozart to play the piano! You might feel awkward at first, because you are a beginner. Set aside your perfectionist performance standards and enjoy the activity for itself, without worrying about how well you perform. Doing it is what matters!

HEALTHY BODY

Chinese medicine takes a preventive approach. For centuries doctors in China were given the task of keeping people healthy and were judged by their ability to prevent illness.

> In ancient China, a first-class physician was one who could not only cure disease, but could also prevent disease. Only a second-class physician had to wait until his patients became ill so he could then treat them when there were obvious symptoms and signs. It is for this reason that the doctor was paid by the patient when he was healthy and the payment was stopped when he was ill. This was so much so that the doctor had to give the patient free of cost the medicines he required, medicines which he, the doctor, had paid for out of his own pocket (Mann 1973, 221).

Chinese doctors believe that by the time disease develops, it is almost too late—just as it would be too late to start digging a well for water when you are already thirsty. Prevention is beginning to become a focus of modern Western medicine as well.

Eastern medicine looks closely at the state of a person's health and makes classifications based on nuances. Chinese doctors notice subtle differences in skin color and eyes. They listen to the patient's voice, observe his or her general level of energy, and even note the appearance of the tongue. All these changes can signal both actual and impending disharmony before it leads to symptoms. A sensitive, skilled practitioner can diagnose current and even former health conditions going back a number of years just from feeling the patient's pulse. In ancient times physicians were forced to diagnose the emperor's concubines by taking a pulse on the wrist, anonymously presented through a curtain, in order to preserve the women's dignity and modesty. The doctor might never see any other part of the woman and yet was expected to correctly diagnose her, treat her, and keep her healthy.

Traditionally a wise practitioner could even predict if an illness was likely to occur in the future. Such pulse readings, almost psychic, are an art, taught by personal apprenticeship. Diagnosis leads to corrective prescription, without the need for invasive empirical tests. Physical changes follow disharmony, in the Eastern model of medicine.

Laypersons are not trained to read the body like a physician, but anyone can become more aware of his or her own inner harmony. Although we live in our bodies, we often ignore our physical experience unless there is a problem. The exercises that follow help use body awareness as a focus of meditation. With awareness and sensitivity to your own body, you can promote good health. You may even help prevent conditions that could lead to illness. This is not an invitation to hypochondria. Be sensitive to the true nature of your sensations, not your worries, fears, and imagination. Please check out any concerns with a doctor.

MEDITATION ON TEMPERATURE I

Sit cross-legged in meditation. Make sure you are in a room that is not too warm or too cold, or perhaps go outdoors when the temperature is comfortable. After several minutes of calm, relaxed breathing, place the palm of your hand over your arm at the elbow. Feel the temperature of your skin. Is it warmer or cooler than your palm? Notice the quality of the temperature. Is it warm or cool, damp or dry? Now place your palm on your forehead and pay attention to how it feels. Compare the temperature sensation. Scan attentively through your body. Notice any areas that are tight. For example, are your shoulders somewhat tense? Check their temperature with your hand. Usually the temperature will be different.

MEDITATION ON TEMPERATURE II

You can use your awareness of temperature to help you. If you are overly warm, you can cool down; or if you are too cold, warm up. First check out any concerns with your doctor if you are suffering from fever, of course. This exercise is a simple remedy to correct an uncomfortable temperature imbalance. Sit comfortably and close your eyes. To warm up, visualize a warm day, a hot fire in a fireplace, or any other image you have of warmth. Focus your attention on this image and wait. An alternative method is to concentrate your attention on a warm area of your skin and imagine the warmth spreading. To cool down, use cold images. You may find that cool compresses or warm hand towels combined with meditation can help you feel comfortable, enhancing your well-being.

Regular meditation is no substitute for getting necessary medical attention, but sometimes you may be able to prevent sickness before it takes hold. Stay in tune with yourself by practicing meditation.

HEALTHY BALANCE: MIND, BODY, SPIRIT

The yin/yang doctrine presumes a balancing process of dynamic equilibrium. Attuned meditators learn to be at one with their surroundings, within and without: an organism in the environment. They restore balance when in disharmony and respond correctly to the interrelationships.

Restoring the correct connection between your body-sense and the outer situation is health-giving. What this means in practical terms according to Chinese medicine is that the body is in balance within, yin and yang, with opposites interacting, e.g., light and heavy, cool and warm, acid and base, and so on. Internal equilibrium is balanced with the external forces of nature, such as heat or coolness. Thus, the individual balance for people when they are adapted to living in a warm climate might be very different from their balance in a cold place. A visit to a cold climate may be initially shocking, to a person from the tropics. Vermonters are warm at temperatures that a Californian might find unpleasant. Conversely, a brisk shower may be stimulating when we feel sluggish and overly warm. When the balance is interrupted, the body tries to restore its equilibrium. The doctor's role is to make the conditions favorable for the body to rebalance itself. *Natura sanat.* Nature heals.

This Eastern concept of balance has its counterpart in Western medicine's concept of homeostasis, which holds that there is an optimum equilibrium within the body, the *interior milieu*. This equilibrium is relatively stable and allows the body to cope with changing external conditions. An organism's tendency to come back into balance was researched extensively by Claude Bernard in the 1850s. Bernard believed that living beings must be considered as a harmonious whole. He recognized the interdependence of social and behavioral life. Bernard's theory was the basis for homeostasis.

Walter B. Cannon, M.D., coined the term *homeostasis* for this natural wisdom of the body. Despite any disturbances, the body finds and maintains its own stability and balance.

Cannon researched the body's many defense mechanisms that help protect us from harm and keep the body stable. He believed that it was almost miraculous that our bodies, which are made of unstable materials, can persist in health for decades. The reason that health is even possible is the perfect balance and harmony of homeostasis.

When there is harmony, health prevails; this harmony is dynamic, not static. Thus, a highly trained, competitive runner requires a different physical adjustment and dynamic balance than does a less active office worker; food intake differs radically, amount of exercise varies greatly, even the amount of inner tissue repair is not the same. Yet, both individuals could be in excellent health. There is a fine art to attuning individuals to their own optimal balance which may diverge from standardized norms. This is akin to "power-tuning" a car, timing and setting it to the octane of gas used and conditions regularly encountered, so that there is less "ping" and better performance.

Inner and outer are not two: as Eastern philosophy teaches us, dualities are to be transcended. But their interrelationship sometimes requires restoring harmony. Disharmony leads to increased stress and potentially ill health. Harmony results in reduced stress and potentially absence of illness. The right balance can lead to a long life with vitality. The exercises that follow are designed to help you find your own balance.

REFLECTION ON BALANCED LIVING I

In this exercise you will explore the balance in your own life with regard to sleeping, eating, working, resting, and exercising. Often we go through our day out of balance, pushing in one direction or another without balancing the forces.

Sit however you feel most comfortable. Close your eyes. Think back over the past day. How much sleep did you get the night before? What kind of food did you have at your meals? How often did you eat and in what quantities? Did you enjoy your food? How long and hard did you work? Did you rest at all? Was there any time for exercise? Then think back over the past week—then the past month and then the past two months. Look for patterns over time. If you notice a large imbalance, note it along with your feelings. Clear your mind of these thoughts when you have come to terms with them, and wait for any other thoughts or feelings to surface.

REFLECTION ON BALANCED LIVING II

If you have begun to recognize imbalances, think about ways to alter them. Often balance can be achieved by making very slight changes. Adding a few minutes of meditation each day can begin to correct an imbalance of stressful overwork. Thomas Edison was a firm believer in fifteen-minute catnaps to recharge his mental batteries. Then he could return to his continuous inventive endeavors with renewed vigor. Fifteen minutes of exercise will help correct a sedentary lifestyle. In China a short session of regular, systematic outdoor exercise, at a fixed period during the day, has helped many people work more comfortably. Try to be moderate in your changes: look for the Middle Way. Find what fits in with your life. Small corrections may make a big difference over time.

CHI: INTERNAL ENERGY

Chinese medicine is based on the concept of chi, an invisible internal energy that circulates through the body via meridians. According to Eastern medicine, the individual balance involves the free flow of chi. When you are ill, your chi has been blocked or stuck, trapped in one area, thereby disrupting its natural flow through your body. Too much or too little chi is not healthy. Properly stimulating key points along the meridian system can unblock or reroute the chi to promote healing. Acupuncture, acupressure, herbs, and massage are all used to restore the flow of chi and thereby bring the patient back to health.

Raising Your Chi

Taoist meditators believe that the lower abdomen is the source of chi energy. The Chinese call this area, located approximately one and a half inches below the navel and one third of the way through the body, the *Dan Tien*. Originally nourished through the umbilical chord, the embryo's energy is circulated from this lower abdominal area. Taoists believe that you can reclaim this source of energy by raising the chi in your abdomen and then circulating it, using your mind.

RAISING CHI MEDITATION

Turn your attention to your lower abdomen and breathe comfortably for several minutes. Bring the air in through your nose, down into your lungs, and then out again. Permit your rib cage to rise and fall slightly, with your abdomen expanding and contracting with each complete breath in and out. Breathe gently as you focus all your attention on this area. You will eventually begin to feel a slight warmth in your lower abdomen. Taoists say that when the spirit moves, the chi moves. Imagine the warmth beginning to spread around to your back, up through your head, and back down to your abdomen, in a circle. Keep your attention moving in this circle through your body. With careful practice, you will feel the warmth, your chi increase.

CIRCULATING THE CHI MEDITATION

Taoism has long combined meditation with slow, steady movement to increase energy and promote health and longevity. This breathing exercise is drawn from the Taoist Chuang-tzu to help you raise your energy level by circulating your chi.

Stand with your feet shoulder-width apart, arms at your sides. Relax your body. Slowly bend your knees, allowing your arms to hang down as you inhale gently. Then slowly and evenly straighten your legs as you raise your arms up over your head, fully extended. Exhale. You can rise up on your toes as you stretch upward if you would like to get more exercise in your legs. Repeat this movement slowly, gently, five or more times. Maintain loose, slow, smooth movements and gentle breathing. Do you feel a tingling or warmth in your arms and legs? Breathe and imagine it circulating.

DYNAMIC BALANCE—POISED FOR ACTION

The centered attitude, in harmony, with chi flowing freely, is the healthy way to live according to Eastern wisdom. The center point of interaction is a poised, dynamic balance, which gives an experience of harmony. Health and correct action clearly follow. When you are centered, you are grounded in your true self, which is at one with your surroundings. Then your reactions to circumstances can accurately reflect what is in your environment.

Being centered is no longer a matter of attempting to adjust to a fixed norm. In our constantly changing culture, norms change before we can adjust to them. Instead, your situation or circumstances now becomes the basis for action, an opportunity to express your enlightenment. Then your reactions make sense and become mature responses. You can work out things and come to terms with the situation's demands from your inner sense of balance. You experience any deficit clearly, in the same way you experience any plus. Your center gives you a reference point from which to judge things.

In physics the stability of an object is improved by properly placing its center of gravity (Watanabe and Avakian 1984, 36). You can see this principle for yourself by tipping a large box slowly on edge. There is a balance point at which the box, even a very heavy box, balances perfectly on edge. But if you continue pushing farther, the center of gravity is too far outside the box, and it can tip over easily. When you throw an opponent in judo, the inertial balance of the opponent must first be broken. If he or she is stable, throwing the opponent is difficult. The key to not allowing yourself to be thrown is to return to the center, to the point where your center of gravity is directly underneath you. In judo a small person can thereby overcome a larger one. If you remain centered and natural, remarkable things can be done.

What does all this mean in practical terms? If you return to the harmony found within your own center, you have some reference point for your life. Disturbance is real and uncomfortable, but you can always return to being centered. Disharmony from illness and conflict will not rock you for long, and it becomes clear how to regain your composure: return to the center. Doing so can affect your business, your relationships, and your health. There is no absolute standard of what this must be for everyone. An energetic, dynamic individual has a different harmony than a quiet intellectual does. Each of us must learn what our personal Way is.

13
THE WAY OUT
OF CONFLICT

The Great Way is calm and large hearted.
For it nothing is easy, nothing is hard.
—from "Hsinhsinming"

T raveling along life's path, there are times when all flows smoothly. You have meditated and developed a calm awareness. Your endeavors work out well and everything is just as you would like it to be. Such ideal experiences are wonderful. But for most of us, these moments are transitory, fleeting. Conflicts inevitably arise and our path seems blocked.

Participating in the world is an important aspect of life. Often as part of accomplishing goals, we engage with others, try to work out the best possible relationship, and cope with problems constructively as they crop up. In our previous book *Living Meditation,* we suggested that pragmatism's value of meliorism, to seek to improve things, is useful. When we open our minds to perceive accurately and sensitively, we can discover what prevents us from evolving fully and accomplishing our true goals. We learn about ourselves in relation to

the world, our limitations and deficiencies, and about the require-
ments of our situation. Through this process, we may develop
strengths and mental skills to help us. If we are fully one with our true
self, we will not be held back by illusion or conflict.

Conflict is not, in and of itself, necessarily bad, especially when
the situation offers a dilemma that may be manageable. Freud believed that conflict was fundamental to human nature. A seemingly
negative situation may present an opportunity from which to learn
and mature. In the process you may discover a higher level of functioning that incorporates both sides of the conflict in a new synthesis.

Conflict resolution demands sincerity and courage to face what
you are truly doing and feeling. With faith and a willingness to work
out matters, the Way will emerge. Only if you are sincere and honestly
search for it does conflict resolution become possible. In a relationship, when both people truly commit themselves to resolving problems, these methods can help. A commitment to the relationship is
primary. Resolution can be rewarding, but a bond is necessary.

Create your own variations on these methods; add them to your
repertoire of conflict-resolution and problem-solving techniques. Experiment with the different approaches presented in this chapter. In
some situations, one method may be appropriate; other circumstances may call for another approach. Let meditation guide you.

PERCEPTIONS' ILLUSIONS

Sorting out difficulties requires a clear perception of the difference between what is and what is not the matter: the true nature of the problem. Sometimes our perceptions are what disturb us, rather than the
problem itself. The wise response is to discern whether what disturbs
us is what it truly is or what we perceive it to be.

We interpret what we experience through our senses. Interpretation is inseparable from perception itself. We see, but the meaning of what we see is affected by our past experience as well as what we think we are perceiving now. We may believe that we see an object when we look at it. For example, this page in front of you seems to be part of a book. But your experience of this book is affected by years of education, including the fact that you now can read these words and derive meaning. You know what a book is and so can put your perception into context. A primitive person, raised outside modern culture, might never have seen a book or not know anything about reading. This individual would not perceive a book the same way we do. This inescapable condition can be used positively. You can comprehend and cope better by creative interpretation through meditation.

The mental side of physical phenomena is inseparable from the reality and actually changes your interpretation. You can improve your attitude for coping with other people by changing your point of view. According to Buddhism, meditation brings us to this realization. As Alan Watts explained:

In sum, then, the Buddhist discipline is to realize that anguish or conflict arises from the grasping of entities singled out from the world by ignore-ance—grasping in the sense of acting or feeling toward them as if they were actually independent of context (Watts 1975, 66).

EXERCISE TO CLARIFY PERCEPTIONS

Decide that during a portion of a particular day you will meditate on at least one sequence of actions. Suppose you pick folding laundry or balancing your checkbook. Before you begin, think carefully about what this task means to you: Do you think of it as an unpleasant chore? Is it a challenge, or do you find it easy? Consider carefully. Clear your mind for several minutes. Then begin the task, clearing your mind of all preconceptions. Approach the action with an open mind, as if it were the first time. Stay attuned throughout, noticing everything as you do it. When you are finished, reflect on the experience. Is there another way to interpret your task now?

WHAT A THING IS AND WHAT IT IS NOT

We should not worry.
About that which is not
Nor be too concerned about
What we have or have not got
Conflict's resolution
Is to awaken from illusion

—C. Alexander Simpkins

Sometimes you can understand what a thing is more clearly if you perceive it in terms of what it is not. Both Gestalt theory and Buddhist philosophy have shown us that things both are and are not. The figure (what a thing is) and background (what a thing is not) are both important in defining its perceived reality. Sometimes it is best to consider what "it is," to solve a conflict. Other times it is better to understand what "it is not," for conflict resolution through creative alternatives. Not-knowing is the beginning of truly knowing. Truly knowing is the beginning of not-knowing.

WHAT IS AND WHAT IS NOT EXERCISE

Sit in meditation for several minutes, clearing your mind of all thoughts. Then think of a situation that bothers you. Perhaps you are unhappy with the way someone in your life is treating you. Or maybe you do not like how a project is going. Dismiss your thoughts about the situation, of what it is. Think about what it is not. For example, if you are considering a relationship, what is the other person not doing? For example, he is not affectionate enough; she is not willing to disclose herself; he does not do enough; or, perhaps, she does too much. After you have considered what the situation is not, ask yourself, What is the other person actually doing now? Returning to our examples, the unaffectionate man leaves you alone; the nondisclosing woman responds shyly with reserve. Although he does not do enough, perhaps he does help on weekends; she may do too much, but she is always there for you. Consider whether your dissatisfaction is based on what the other person is doing, or on what the other is not doing. Conversely, are you annoyed because of what you are doing or not doing in the relationship? Are you doing your part? Is the disturbance based on what is, or on what is not?

PERSONAL STYLES OF CONFLICT RESOLUTION

People vary in how they deal with conflict. Some people want to face the situation immediately, plunging directly into the center of conflict until it is resolved. But others find such an approach overwhelming, even a bit threatening. They become more defensive and uncomfortable. These people step away, or ask the other to step away, to gather themselves and calm down, thereby allowing them to return to the dilemma later and find resolution. Sometimes one person's style of coping may be mismatched with a partner who uses the opposite style, making communication and agreement difficult. Awareness can help you both be more compassionate and flexible with each other. The following exercise will help you discern your own natural style of conflict resolution so that you can work things out.

REFLECTION ON CONFLICT RESOLUTION

For this exercise you will reflect on the form of the argument, not its content. Think back on a time you were engaged in an argument that mattered, with someone you care about. Did you feel like getting away in order to calm down, or did you feel a tense need, a feeling of urgency to address the problem immediately? What about the other person? Did the other have similar tendencies? Observe and consider these qualities about yourself and your partner. Sometimes conflicts are prolonged because two people have different natural tendencies for timing. You may learn from recalling other instances with other people, to compare and gain a sense of your personal style.

Sometimes the stress of attempting to resolve differences, or the suffering and feelings involved, are too much. You may need time and space. Ask for them to gather your best resources. Or offer time and space to the other person as an invitation to reconsider things more maturely later. Dignity and calmness in conflict may offer an opportunity for change. Later on, you may feel able to return to your dialogue, renewed and ready to resolve your differences. Feelings change. Matters may then be open to negotiation. Disharmony dissolves and harmony is reestablished. Then you can work together on what you are attempting to accomplish. Interpersonal harmony is an extension of individual harmony.

THE ROOTS OF CONFLICT

By going one step farther back in thought, discordant opinions are reconciled by being seen to be two extremes of one principle (Emerson 1926, 217).

Conflict resolved by force or domination is always temporary; it will eventually break down when force dissipates or domination evolves or is removed. Conflict resolved by harmonious settlement, one that addresses the true cause of the conflict, can be lasting. A new relationship ultimately emerges. Everyone learns something, everyone grows, and differences are no longer as they were.

MEDITATION ON THE ROOTS OF CONFLICT

To resolve conflict, it may be necessary to follow actions to their roots, to understand their source. Often conflict is viewed as simply a problem in conduct, requiring the strong arm of discipline—strict control of behavior is used to solve the problem. But this approach is only a superficial manifestation, temporary in its effects. What can be done instead? First consider the underlying basis for action. The true conflict, the genuine, must be accepted as the center and be addressed, not just the outer manifestation. For example, when children misbehave, look deeper. What are they expressing? Are they getting attention by making a fuss? Do they feel hungry or tired but are unable to express themselves? Look beyond the obvious to the true nature of the problem.

FLEXIBLE ACTION: MOUNTAIN SEA CHANGE

Who leaves all receives more.

—Ralph Waldo Emerson

Sometimes you may find that the conflict does not get resolved. The greater the effort, the less the progress. Somehow one or the other cannot come to an acceptable agreement. When there seems to be no possible solution, you may have become entangled in spirit. This water technique, adapted from Miyamoto Musashi, the Japanese swordsman-philosopher, can help. This insightful technique transcends its original context.

MOUNTAIN SEA CHANGE MEDITATION

Instead of continuing with the same approach, withdraw for a moment. Sit down and close your eyes. Clear your mind of the difficulty. You can use any number of meditation exercises from Part II. Change your spirit. For example, if you have been strongly insisting on a straight-on encounter, what would a more circular approach be like? Create a new alternative. When you feel that your spirit is changed, re-engage your efforts, but from the new perspective. Meditation can help you discover different alternatives. What is important is to resolve matters, not to stubbornly enforce some particular point.

VARIATION ON MOUNTAIN SEA CHANGE EXERCISE

As in the previous exercise, first withdraw from your frustrated efforts by meditating. Then, instead of repeating the same thing over and over without success, consider doing the opposite. If you are seeking a solution by reasoning things out, try your intuition. If you are passionately engaged, step back and calm down, then try again. If calm, cool logic is not working, draw upon your emotions. If you are unable to advance, try retreating, letting things be. Then resolution takes place, naturally. Even if the opposite is not exactly correct, new possibilities will occur to you.

NONCONTENDING

The Taoist response is to conform to the demands of the problematic situation by staying with it, decisively flexible yet fluid, springy and yielding.

You can enhance your sensitivity with this exercise. It can be useful for interacting with others sensitively. Do the exercise that follows and then think of it as a metaphor for conflict. Can you stay attuned without contending?

CHI-SAO EXERCISE IN NONCONTENDING

Face your partner. Let your partner be the guide, and you be the one to follow, sensitively. Stand a few feet away, facing each other. Your partner raises one arm, bent at the elbow, extending the hand forward. Raise and place your hand lightly over the wrist of the other and close your eyes. Your partner moves his or her semi-relaxed arm around slowly, extending back and forth, up and down. You stay with your partner's hand, lightly moving in unison. Can you sense the force of movement without adding any force of your own?

After several minutes, switch roles. You lead, and your partner follows. Repeat the exercise with the other hand as well. Both people should remain relaxed at all times.

This exercise illustrates what the Taoists mean by noncontending: to be aware, in touch with what is happening, following carefully, without changing the course of things, yet permitting change to take place if it happens. The yielding response does not require that you completely withdraw or pull back in retreat if you are obstructed or blocked. Respect the flow of events and wait for the appropriate moment to respond again, when the resisting, contending force has spent itself somewhat. Every force contains the seeds of its counterforce.

We are not separate from the world; we are always part of it, interacting. "The organism of man does not confront the world but is in the world" (Watts 1975, 70). We must take our environment into account in our actions. Change is part of the dynamic flow of life. All we need to do is allow it.

GOALLESS ACHIEVEMENT

Therefore the Sage
Puts himself in the background; but is always to the fore.
Remains outside; but is always there.
Is it not just because he does not strive for any personal end
That all his personal ends are fulfilled?
　　　　　　　　—*Tao Te Ching*, Book VII, translated by Waley

By yielding flexibly, we can meet difficult challenges and resolve situations without our trying to achieve a goal. The fluid technique influenced by Taoism is one of flowing with the situation and remaining within it, without committing to gaining or losing anything.

YIELDING ONE SMALL THING EXERCISE

When you are trying to come to terms with something important or attempting to achieve interpersonal cooperation, ask yourself, what really matters? What are you willing to yield? What can you give, without compromising the main purpose or objective? What is your response to this? Is it workable? Yield just enough—begin with one small but significant thing—while following the dynamics of the situation carefully, and a very positive outcome may emerge: cooperation.

TO GAIN IS TO LOSE AND
TO LOSE IS TO GAIN

Sometimes when we communicate unsuccessfully, we are so intent on winning the argument that any victory is a costly one. We win the battle but lose greatly in the process. Next time you are in an argument, attune yourself to the other person's communications, much as you did with the other's movements in chi-sao. Listen carefully to what the other person is saying. Stay with his or her logic, thoughts, feelings. As you do so, maintain self-awareness of your own feelings and thoughts, but do not let your own perspective engulf you. Shift back to the other. Can you imagine his or her point of view and perceptions—as real to the other as yours are to you? Often when the other person is truly experienced, not just listened to, he or she will be more open to you as well. Communication can flow, and the differences may be resolved naturally—if you can determine together how to work it out to restore balance for both. Sometimes one or the other, or even both, must lose so that both may win.

BEYOND CONFLICT

> *The perfect Way (Tao) is without difficulty,*
> *Save that it avoids picking and choosing...*
> *If you want to get the plain truth,*
> *Be not concerned with right and wrong.*
> *The conflict between right and wrong*
> *Is the sickness of the mind.*
>
> —"Hsinhsinming"

Many conflicts are illusions. Yoga, Buddhism, and Taoism recognize that ultimately, all is One. Thus, the choices we make, the sides we take, are but different aspects of the whole. Zen purists explain this idea radically—there is no discrimination to be made. But in our own lives, in the day-to-day world, the advice of Alan Watts might be more feasible: "It is simply that in a universe of relativity all choosing, all taking of sides, is playful" (Watts 1975, 163). When you meditate, conflict dissolves into the Oneness of your deeper self, your original mind, true nature. Find the dynamic balance point. Conflict both is and is not, neither is nor is not. Your true nature is beyond conflict.

土屋右衛門

Twenty-four Warriors of Koyo
Tosa Mitsunori, Japanese, 1583-1638
Ink and color on silk, early 17th century
Gift of the Asian Arts Committee

14
INNER STRENGTH AND SPIRITUAL DISCIPLINE

*Everyone is endowed with body and mind, though
their actions inevitably vary, being either strong or
weak, brave or cowardly. It is through the daily
actions of our body and mind, however, that we
directly become enlightened. This is known as the
realization of the Way.*

—Dogen, Japanese Zen master

S trength is more than a conditioned body; strength comes from a strong spirit. Being tough and strong, both physically and mentally, is as valued in the East as it is in the West. But people develop strength differently in the East.

In the West, the Marines are known for their toughness. They train hard under strict discipline and spartan conditions to become strong and thereby capable of withstanding even the most arduous circumstances. From the Eastern perspective, toughness and strength are not just about conditioning and making one's body impervious to pain. The Eastern approach to strengthening combines physical challenge with sensitivity. Properly cultivated, the two together build strength of spirit and body.

CHALLENGE

In Japan the tradition of strengthening the spirit continues today in a modernized form. It is customary for businessmen to go on retreats together for the purpose of toughening the spirit. Natural settings are used symbolically, to inspire and reawaken people's inner sensitivity. The participants might sit under a waterfall, the cold water cascading down their backs as they engage in calming meditation. Sometimes they climb a mountain for the experience of meeting a difficult challenge together. The entire company might go on a long, exhausting run along a difficult path. The businessmen engage in deep meditation to remain sensitively aware throughout the experience. They also share a good time together.

EXERCISE IN TOUGHENING

Take on a personally meaningful recreational, physical challenge. If you are athletic, you might take a hike out in nature, go white-water rafting, or perhaps go rock climbing with a trained group. For the homemaker, you could choose to undertake a major overhaul of your house. A musician could take on an extended practice session. Whatever you choose, make it meaningful and safe.

As you are performing the challenge, keep your mind clear by meditating. Stay with each action by meditating on your sensations. Do not let your mind wander. At the end of the day, sit quietly for a time, meditating to absorb and contemplate what the challenge means to you, and experience how you feel.

SENSITIVITY

Combining sensitivity with hard training has been part of Eastern martial arts for centuries. The Hwa Rang Do, an elite military group in ancient Korea, worked out ferociously in order to be physically strong and capable. Yet they also studied Confucian classics, philosophy, and poetry to develop their spirit.

The stereotype of the samurai of feudal Japan as an insensitive brute is similarly inaccurate. Gentleness and sensitivity were combined with strength and daring: "The bravest are the tenderest, the loving are the daring" (Nitobe 1973, 32). This point is an important aspect of strengthening the spirit: the spirit that endures is also sensitive, even passionate. Passion and sensitivity were expressed often (even in the midst of battle) through songs and poetry. It was customary for a samurai to compose a poem as he died on the battlefield, to show that he could be simultaneously fearless in the face of death and also sensitive to his moment of passing. The farewell poem of the samurai Nyudo, spoken just before he died, follows:

Holding forth this sword,
I cut vacuity in twain;
In the midst of the great fire,
A stream of refreshing breeze!
(From Suzuki 1973, 84)

Haiku was often the style of poetry the samurai used to express the intensity of battle. Because of its simplicity and directness, haiku arouses the deepest awareness of everyday life. Here are a few examples from Zen monk Basho (1643–94), one of the greatest haiku poets:

When the lightning flashes,
How admirable he who thinks not—
"Life is fleeting."

The old pond.
A frog jumps in.
Plop!

(From Ross, 1960, 124-25)

Today, Westerners also write haiku. The strict adherence to syllables that is so appropriate to the Japanese language has been loosened to accommodate English. The poems below are examples of English language haiku, with themes familiar to contemporary life.:

Cool rain trickles down
Quiet music soothes the street
Peaceful emptiness

—C. Alexander Simpkins

On the beach we walk
In waves we find our balance
Lost in the moment

—C. Alexander Simpkins

Shadows grow longer
One Life's battlefield
Yet still we stand

—C. Alexander Simpkins

EXERCISE IN POETRY WRITING

Like the samurai of ancient Japan, you can capture the moment in poetry with awareness and sensitivity. After you have taken on a challenge, write a poem that expresses your experience. Meditate on the challenge that you underwent. Bring the experience vividly to your awareness. Then write what comes to mind.

If you would like to write your poem as a haiku, the rules are simple: three lines without rhyme, approximately five syllables in the first line, seven in the second, and five in the third. The haiku should express your direct experience of a particular moment out in nature as if it is happening in the present, not looking back on it.

DISCIPLINE

Just continue in your calm, ordinary practice and your character will be built up.

—Shunryu Suzuki

Discipline, in the sense we usually understand the word, is imposed by authority and control. In Zen and Taoism, this external source is believed to be false. True discipline comes from within and beyond you. Discipline arises within unity with a greater reality: greater than any one person, situation, or action.

ZEN DISCIPLINE

In Zen, discipline is letting go to the unconscious, to the absolute principle, not imposing your own will from outside. Discipline is a natural consequence of recognizing the truth of what is. Your part in the whole becomes clear, you know what to do, and action follows. All efforts come from the being of the mind itself. Discipline is not something that can be added.

Those who have no definite faith in this, that Mind is the Buddha, and attempt an achievement by means of a discipline attached to form, are giving themselves up to wrong imagination; they deviate from the right path (Suzuki 1960, 113).

EXERCISE IN ZEN DISCIPLINE

Zen discipline derives directly from meditation, in which the discovery of mind takes place. In a Zen monastery, meditation is done every day without fail. Then, as the Buddha-mind emerges, self-discipline develops naturally.

Pick a certain time of the day to be your meditation time. Set aside a certain length of time to sit quietly in meditation. You can perform the zazen meditation in Part II or pick any other meditation from this book. Most important of all is to meditate every day, without fail, at the exact same hour, for the allotted time. Some days you might not feel like meditating. You must meditate anyway, no matter how you feel or what is happening in your life. This is the Zen form of discipline. In time, you will reap the benefits.

Bushido required self-control and self-restraint from the samurai. They were expected to control and limit their reactions. Their aim was to find the balance point. Composure or poise requires dignified restraint in expression. Nitobe believed that Greek stoicism is a parallel. Quieting the emotions was a characteristic response of the samurai to emotionally stimulating events, so they could react with dignity and poise.

Zen Buddhism further clarifies the place of feelings. Feelings should not be interfered with, but do not make an object out of them.

> The emotive state by itself is abnormal and contrary to satori; emotion itself is normal and not contrary to satori. But it is a thousand times easier to perceive the emotions than the existence of the emotive state. And so man often believes that it is good to curb the emotions, and all his work is in vain because it is misdirected (Benoit 1990, 124).

We are all bothered by troubling emotional states and moods at times. But viewing moods and emotions as a state is the root of the problem, not the feelings themselves. When you allow yourself to feel fully, in the midst of experiencing your emotions, you can be at ease with them. Emotions are not a bothersome state, a problem or stumbling block. Rather, they are an important part of your attunement, part of the spectrum of your awareness. If you delete your emotions, you are missing an important part of your orientation.

EXERCISE WITH EMOTIONS

Zen teaches us to be aware of emotion without judgment—no concepts. Often people find emotions difficult to handle because of the secondary judgments that they form about their feelings. The Zen way is to feel the emotion, attentively, without conceptualizing. Then the feeling does not become fixed as an emotional state but remains a flowing process.

Sit in meditation, calmly and quietly, for several minutes. Now think about a situation that affects you personally, one that you have feelings about. Perhaps you care about a person, or maybe something at work or school disturbs you. Perhaps you prefer to visualize or hear the voice of the person. Stay with the feelings as you notice the details of it. Do you also have physical sensations at the same time? For example, if you feel nervous about something, you may have an uneasy feeling in your stomach (butterflies). Do not indulge in any condemnations or judgments about it, such as "I feel angry, and that's bad; people should not make me angry," or "they should not do that, so I feel angry." Stay with the emotion for several minutes, and try to let go of any fixed reaction. Then relax again before you stop meditating. Leave room for meditation's calm.

TAOIST DISCIPLINE

Using yin-yang theory, opposites neutralize each other. Taoists exercise discipline in coping with a situation by yielding to the nature of things by accepting them and finding a way to permit conditions to neutralize themselves. Discipline becomes effortless as the Taoist becomes one with the problem. The best course is to redirect or step out of the way. Do not butt your head against the wall of circumstance. Instead, yield and flow with it.

Taoists apply this strategy in many ways, always seeking the balance, the center. Holistic medicine is an example.

Softness, apparent weakness, is the path to discipline and then to success.

> *Can you educate your soul so that it encompasses the*
> *One without dispersing itself?*
> *Can you make your strength unitary and achieve that*
> *softness that makes you like a little child?*
> —Tao Te Ching, Book X, translated by Wilhelm

TAOIST DISCIPLINE EXERCISE

Perform the previous meditation but stay with your feelings. Do not judge them and do not try to change them in any way. Go with the flow, relaxing your muscles if you can. Let your emotion be, maintaining your awareness, moment to moment, but also remaining as calm as possible. Thus, if you are sad, stay with this feeling, flow with it as if you are following a current. Do not fight against what you feel. Express it, if you need to. In staying with your feeling, you will gradually notice that the feeling alters. Perhaps you do not feel quite as sad. You may discover other meanings. Often, in going with a feeling instead of fighting against it, the emotion resolves and dissipates.

If you have tried the exercises in this section and found that staying with your emotions is too difficult, too painful or disturbing, it is possible that you have a conflict that requires attention. If so, you may be helped by psychotherapy. Good therapy can help resolve emotional conflicts that form obstructions to your natural, intuitive mind. Usually psychotherapy can be initiated over a brief period, to set the process in motion. Carefully choose a person whom you feel comfortable talking to, a therapist who is sympathetic to personal growth and Eastern philosophy. Then your meditation can work with the process. As you deal with emotional difficulties, you will continue along your meditative Path to discover your own unique enlightened Way.

15
THE WAY TO DO
THE CORRECT THING

The superior man thinks of virtue; the small man thinks of comfort.

—Confucius, The Analects

I f we do not make an ethical commitment, we travel the Path in darkness. Buddhists require all initiates to take certain vows to guide their conduct. Dogen said, "How can you expect to become a Buddha or patriarch if you do not guard against faults and prevent yourself from doing wrong?" (Dogen, in Yokoi 1990, 84.) When you do the correct thing, the perfect Way stretches before you, without boundaries or obstructions.

HUMILITY

The Master said, "The superior man has a dignified ease without pride. The mean man has pride without a dignified ease."

—Confucius, Analects

Confucianism, Taoism, and Buddhism teach that the humble person is the truly wise one. Confucius said in the *Analects,* "The firm, the enduring, the simple, and the modest are near to virtue" (Legge 1971, 274).

The virtue of humility, central to becoming a monk or training in traditional martial arts, keeps the personality in balance. Humility is the absence of pride. But humility and pride are actually two sides of the same coin.

Great accomplishment calls for dynamic balance within the person. Achievement requires the humility to receive and respond to criticism along with the faith in self to continue on, incorporating criticism and modifying behavior accordingly. Both humility and pride have their place.

Emptiness is the basis for enlightenment. The utility of a vessel is in its emptiness. Empty space is not a vacuum, a hollow nothingness. Instead, emptiness is the fertile void of possibility, the white spaces in the figure-ground, the silence between notes in a melody, the space within an atom. Only from emptiness can true understanding spring.

With wisdom comes the recognition that there is always more to learn. As Confucius said, "Shall I teach you what knowledge is? When you know a thing, to hold that you know it; and when you do not know a thing, to allow that you do not know it—this is knowledge" (Legge 1971, 151). Learning is a graduated process. Earning a black belt in martial arts, for example, is not the end but only the beginning of another level, a more advanced realm of understanding. Similarly, becoming enlightened is not the final achievement, the goal, but rather a stepping-stone to a wiser, more compassionate life. If you are too sure of yourself, where is there room for progress? If you have no faith in yourself, what is the basis for your doing?

EXERCISE IN HUMILITY

You can give yourself an experience in humility to help you find your own balance. Pick a community-service project that interests you or is special to you, and volunteer your time. It could be serving dinner to the poor, helping out on a building project with an organization like Habitat for Humanity, talking to patients at a retirement community, or volunteering at a hospital. If you cannot find anything to do in the larger community, begin in your very own neighborhood. Anywhere that can use your help is a good place to start, even on your own street. Put on gloves, bring out a broom and bag, and clean up the outdoor area near where you live. How far can you extend this effort comfortably? As you go through the experience, allow yourself to be fully attentive. Pay attention to the details of your actions as you perform them. Notice how you feel at the time, and then how you feel afterward.

SINCERITY

According to Confucius, sincerity is one of the highest virtues. By meeting life with sincerity, all becomes possible. Elbert Hubbard—American lecturer, publisher, editor, and essayist—believed in sincerity. He said, "Every man who succeeds in anything wins through unflinching, tireless loyalty to that particular thing" (Hubbard 1928, 112). This brings to mind the intensity of Zen, sincerely and wholeheartedly following the Way. Loyalty to life's chosen tasks, with full commitment and total immersion, helps unmeasurably in accomplishing things.

Care and patience in small things becomes mastery in larger things in life, as well. Therefore, the small is the doorway to the greater.

There is a natural concern for the social and moral order, for they reflect the larger harmony of the universe. If the apparently trivial details of life are ignored, then the larger whole suffers, too. The whole is implied in its parts, as the Gestalt psychologists have shown. We all share from birth a common nature that is filled with potential. By our practice, by what we do, we become noble or ignoble, high or low. Choosing the best possible actions is the key to activating potential. Fulfilling potential requires sincerely following the proper course of action, once we know what it is. Values are expressed and found in action, both guiding it and being discovered in it.

In Western thought, we guide our action by values. But actually the two are inseparable. Values are expressed in our everyday actions, even the small ones.

REFLECTION ON THE SMALL I

Think of a small thing that you care about doing, perhaps an obligation, something you should honestly and correctly address and accomplish but somehow do not. What do you feel about doing or not doing it? What prevents you from doing it? Can you take the time to carefully imagine and describe to yourself or even to a good friend how you would accomplish it? What does it mean to you to complete it? How would you feel if you did? Contemplate this sincerely.

REFLECTION ON THE SMALL II

Next set up the circumstances to actually make accomplishing it possible. Can you now follow through? If not, what obstructs you or interferes? Is it inner concerns—for example, doubts, insecurities, or fears? Is it apathy, laziness, or lack of motivation? Is it outer circumstances? Is the task too boring to spend time doing? Are you far too busy to find time for this small project? Are there other concerns? Now, having considered all these potential difficulties, can you set them all aside and just do it?

If actions are performed wholeheartedly, not halfway, thought and action become one. To do things wholeheartedly, not half way—this is how to be truthful in thought and action. Sincerity leads to wholehearted devotion and involvement. As Blyth said:

True meditation is to devote oneself to a thing and understand it, that is, not thinking first and practicing afterwards, but thinking and practice as one activity (Blyth 1960, 28).

EXERCISE IN SINCERE ACTIVITY

Pick something that you enjoy doing. It could be a hobby like painting, building models, collecting, computer rendering, or playing a sport. As you begin the activity, perform it with wholehearted effort, doing each part of the action with care, and making a sincere effort to stay focused. If you are playing tennis, for example, be one with each movement, each experience of what you feel in your stroke, your stance. If you are painting, think only of the painting, the paints, the brush. Be fully attentive to what you are doing as you do it. Be at one with your actions. Try to notice when your attention is drawn to

> **Exercise in Sincere Activity, continued**
>
> something distracting. Then return to focus, as you can. Whatever you choose to do, for the amount of time you have set aside, be wholehearted and sincere in your effort to do it well and completely.
>
> If you are successful with this exercise, you might want to challenge yourself with something more difficult. Try to apply the same wholehearted devotion to a task that is more difficult for you, one you might not enjoy doing or not want to do. Devote yourself to something you have to do in your work or daily chores. Each action matters. Even the most seemingly humble or difficult task has value when done fully and sincerely. No task is too small.

NARROW THE PATH

Samurai training was imbued with the spirit of tenacity. Relentless, day in–day out practice calls forth this spiritual quality. Zen monks consider true enlightenment inseparable from practice—that is, doing meditation. It is through expression in action that ethical values come to life. Once you have a clear understanding of what to do, your Path must be followed sincerely.

Zen arts take people along a creative path. Martial arts, Zen archery, flower arrangement, calligraphy, tea ceremony—all are followed with a resolute intensity, whereby mind, body, and spirit act as one with the art. Many actions in life can be performed with the intensity of a Zen art. But what if conflict arises? Can you deal with conflict and still remain on your Path?

Sometimes, to be productive, you may find that leaving the Path is counterproductive. A resolute mind is essential for change. You must follow through, take the proper steps. Walk the Path that you have seen must be walked, regardless of the initial travails. This is sometimes hard, but it will get easier. If you are having difficulty focusing at work, at school, or in your home life, try the meditation below:

EXERCISE TO NARROW THE PATH

Pick a simple task that you have difficulty doing, either at home, at work, or at school. Begin with one that you can accomplish in less than an hour. Ready yourself by clearing your mind in meditation. Then perform the task with all your attention on what you are doing. If you begin to ruminate, take note of what you think and feel; even write it down if you can, or perhaps tape-record it. Gently bring your thoughts back to what you are doing. Keep all your attention focused on the action and on nothing else. Perform each part of the task as fully as you can. When you are finished, sit quietly and review what you did. Find a natural rhythm that allows you to stay on the Path while also respecting, considering, and dealing with difficulties.

WIDEN THE PATH

Sometimes the Path is not clear. We try to force ourselves to be disciplined. Correctly assessing what actually matters is important. Balance helps. "The superior man, in the world, does not set his mind either for anything, or against anything; what is right he will follow" (Confucius in Legge 1971, 168).

EXERCISE TO WIDEN YOUR PATH

Rigidly holding yourself to only one planned objective is not the only meaning of tenacity. Paradoxically, flexibility can be an important aspect of tenacity. A determined, intense commitment includes more than just absolute resolve.

If the Path you have chosen becomes too narrow, too restricting, a creative approach might help. Consider your personal life's Path. Perhaps it is a career that you are pursuing or a skill you are learning. If you have been faltering on your career path, taking it very seriously yet unable to stay focused, try thinking of it as a hobby. What if you were doing it for fun rather than struggling with serious demands? Can you imagine this, in fantasy? It can be helpful to leave room for the unplanned, the spontaneous, the intuitive. Your attitude affects your experience and your performance. When you are having fun, action may flow effortlessly. Sometimes a straight line is not the best way to get there. Nature's lines are never perfectly straight. Life's edges are curved, uneven.

You may decide that you need a bit of unrelated activity, to find your balance. Sometimes too concentrated an effort is exhausting, such as studying for many hours. If so, experiment with actually doing something different. Perhaps you will realize that this is just a distraction and feel eager to return to your serious Path. Be sensitive to your needs and rhythms. Talk it over with an important person in your life. Experiment, evaluate, and then return to your Path, which may require widening.

The ability to do the correct thing lies within each person. The Way to do what you value is found by choosing the correct action and staying with it faithfully. "Dig within. There lies the wellsprings of good: Ever dig and it will ever flow" (Aurelius 1981, 115).

CONCLUSION

Life's difficulties are resolved in action, not just thought about as mere theoretical problems. Meditation can help us lessen the gap between thinking and acting by giving each its place in the unity. Obstructions dissolve and situations resolve themselves naturally. You become whole, your being and doing united as One. In this unity, the threads of your individual acts can weave satisfying, fulfilling patterns within the tapestry of everyday life.

What, then, does following meditation's Way mean for you? Meditation can link you to your capacity for inward calm as a resource when you need it. You can be strong but still sensitive; the two work together. Your ideas need not bind and encase you: you can always let go of limiting conceptions when necessary. Flexibly yielding does not mean giving in. It often leads to working things out. You will discover your personal, dynamic equilibrium, correctly balanced for you. Find your own central harmony and you will create integration between your inner Way and the outer Way that you must follow. All the actions of your life matter when performed with the wholehearted-ness of meditation. Only by sincerely being and expressing your true nature can you fulfill your destiny, as thought flows smoothly to action.

> *We cannot say*
> *Where your search will end up*
> *But if you meditate*
> *And empty mind's cup*
> *With faith and trust*
> *You will leave doubt behind*
> *Knowledge springs from enlightened wisdom*
> *Seek and you shall find.*
>
> —C. Alexander Simpkins

BIBLIOGRAPHY

Aurelius, Marcus. Translated by Maxwell Staniforth. *Meditations*. New York: Penguin Books, 1981.

Beck, L. A. *The Story of Oriental Philosophy.* 1928. Reprint, New York: New Home Library, 1942.

Benoit, H. *Zen and the Psychology of Transformation: The Supreme Doctrine.* Rochester, Vt: Inner Traditions International, 1990.

Bhikshu. *Karma Yoga.* Chicago: Yogi Publication Society, 1928.

Blofeld, J., trans. *The Zen Teaching of Huang-po.* Boston: Shambhala, 1994.

Blyth, R. H. *Zen and Zen Classics.* Vol. 1. San Francisco: Hokuseido Press, 1960.

————*Zen and Zen Classics.* Vol. 2. San Francisco: Hokuseido Press, 1964.

Brooks, C. *Sensory Awareness: The Discovery of Experiencing.* Santa Barbara, Calif.: Ross Erikson Publishers, 1982.

Chan, W. T. *A Source Book in Chinese Philosophy.* Princeton, N.J.: Princeton University Press, 1963.

Combs, A. W. *Helping Relationships.* Boston: Allyn & Bacon, 1978.

————. *A Theory of Therapy.* Newbury Park, Calif.: Sage Publications, 1989.

Conze, E. *Buddhism: Its Essence and Development.* New York: Philosophical Library, 1951.

————. *A Short History of Buddhism.* Oxford, England: Oneworld Publications, 1995.

Conze, E., I. B. Horner, D. Snellgrove, and A. Waley, eds. *Buddhist Texts Through the Ages.* Oxford, England: Oneworld Publications, 1995.

Dumoulin, H. *Zen Buddhism: A History, India and China.* New York: Macmillan, 1988.

————. *Zen Buddhism: A History, Japan.* New York: Macmillan, 1990.

Duyvendak, J. J. L. *Tao Te Ching: The Book of the Way and Its Virtue.* Boston: Charles E. Tuttle Co., 1996.

Emerson, R. W. *Essays by Ralph Waldo Emerson*. New York: Thomas Y. Crowell, 1926.

Fogarty, J., trans. *A Barefoot Doctor's Manual: The American Translation of the Official Chinese Paramedical Manual*. Philadelphia: Running Press, 1977.

Frank, J. and J. B. Frank. *Persuasion and Healing*. Baltimore: Johns Hopkins University Press, 1991.

Frank, J., R. Hoehn-Saric, S. Imber, B. Liberman, and A. Stone. *Effective Ingredients of Successful Psychotherapy*. New York: Bruner/Mazel, Publishers, 1978.

Fudler, S. *The Tao of Medicine*. Rochester, Vt.: Destiny Books, 1989.

Fung Yu-Lan. *A Short History of Chinese Philosophy*. New York: Free Press, 1966.

Funakoshi, G. *Karate Do*. Tokyo: Kodansha Internationl, 1973.

Graham, Dom Aelred. *The End of Religion*. New York: Harcourt Brace Jovanovich, 1971.

———.*Zen Catholicism*. New York: Harcourt Brace Jovanovich, 1963.

Goldstein, K. *Human Nature in the Light of Psychopathology*. New York: Schocken Books, 1966.

Henderson, H. G. *Haiku in English*. Rutland, Vt.: Charles E. Tuttle Co., 1967.

Herrigel, E. *The Method of Zen*. New York: Vintage, 1960.

Hubbard, E. *Preachments*. Vol. 4. East Aurura, Illinois: Royerafters, 1928.

Hucker, C. O. *China's Imperial Past*. Stanford, Calif.: Stanford University Press, 1975.

James, W. *Principles of Psychology*. 2 vols. New York: Henry Holt and Company, 1896.

Legge, J. *Confucius: Confucian Analects, The Great Learning and the Doctrine of the Mean*. New York: Dover, 1971.

———.*The Texts of Taoism*. 2 vols. New York: Dover, 1962.

Liu, D. *T'ai Chi Ch'uan and Meditation*. New York: Schocken Books, 1986.

Mann, F. *Acupuncture: The Ancient Art of Healing and How It Works Scientifically*. New York: Vintage, 1973.

Maslow, A. H. *Motivation and Personality*. New York: Harper & Row, 1954.

Masunaga, R. *A Primer of Soto Zen*. Honolulu: University of Hawaii Press, 1971.

Moore, C. A. *The Chinese Mind: Essentials of Chinese Philosophy and Culture*. Honolulu: University of Hawaii Press, 1986.

Musashi, M. *The Book of Five Rings: A Guide to Strategy*. Woodstock, N.Y.: Overlook Press, 1974.

Nitobe, I. *Bushido: The Soul of Japan*. Boston: Charles E. Tuttle Co., 1969.

Palos, S. *The Chinese Art of Healing*. New York: Bantam, 1972.

BIBLIOGRAPHY

Parulski, G. *A Path to Oriental Wisdom: Introductory Studies in Eastern Philosophy.* Burbank, Calif.: Ohara Publications, 1976.

Perls, F. S. *Gestalt Therapy Verbatim.* Lafayette, Calif.: Real People Press, 1969.

Perls, F. S., R. E. Hefferline, and P. Goodman. *Gestalt Therapy.* New York: Dell, 1951.

Pine, R. *The Zen Teaching of Bodhidharma.* San Francisco: North Point Press, 1989.

Price, A. F. and W. Mou-Lam. *The Diamond Sutra and the Sutra of Hui-Neng.* Boston: Shambhala, 1990.

Ramacharaka, Y. *A Series of Lessons in Raja Yoga.* Chicago: Yoga Publication Society, 1934.

Reps, P. *Zen Flesh, Zen Bones.* Rutland, Vt.: Charles E. Tuttle Co., 1994.

Rogers, C.R. *A Way of Being.* Boston: Houghton Mifflin Co., 1980.

Ross, N. W., ed. *The World of Zen: An East-West Anthology.* New York: Vintage, 1960.

Sadler, A. L. *Cha-no-yu: The Japanese Tea Ceremony.* Rutland, Vt.: Charles E. Tuttle Co., 1967.

Selye, H. *Stress Without Distress.* New York: Signet, 1974.

———.*The Stress of Life.* New York: McGraw-Hill, 1976.

Simpkins, C. A. and A. M. Simpkins. *Principles of Meditation: Eastern Wisdom for the Western Mind.* Boston: Charles E. Tuttle Co., 1996.

———.*Living Meditation: From Principle to Practice:* Boston: Charles E. Tuttle Co., 1997.

———.*Zen Around the World: A 2500-Year Journey from the Buddha to You.* Boston: Charles E. Tuttle Co., 1997.

———.*Principles of Self Hypnosis: Pathways to the Unconcious.* New York: Irvington, 1991.

Suzuki, D. T. *Essays in Zen Buddhism* (First Series). New York: Grove Press, 1978.

———.*Manual of Zen Buddhism.* New York: Grove Weidenfeld, 1960.

———.*Zen and Japanese Culture.* Princeton, N.J.: Princeton University Press, 1973.

———.*Zen Mind, Beginner's Mind: Informal Talks on Zen Meditation and Practice.* New York: Weatherhill, 1979.

Takuan, S. *The Unfettered Mind.* Tokyo: Kodansha International, 1986

Waddell, N. *The Unborn: The Life and Teachings of Zen Master Bankei 1622–1693.* San Francisco: North Point Press, 1984.

Watanabe, J. and L. Avakian. *Secrets of Judo.* Rutland, Vt.: Charles E. Tuttle Co., 1984.

Watson, B. *The Zen Teachings of Master Lin-Chi*. Boston: Shambhala, 1993.

Watts, A. *The Way of Zen*. New York: Vintage, 1957.

———.*Psychotherapy East and West*. New York: Vintage, 1975.

Welch, H. *Taoism: The Parting of the Way*. Boston: Beacon Press, 1965.

Wilhelm, R. *Tao Te Ching: The Book of Meaning and Life*. London: Penguin Books, 1990.

Wolff, H. G. *Stress and Disease*. Springfield, Ill.: Charles C. Thomas, 1953.

Yokoi, Y. *Zen Master Dogen*. New York: Weatherhill, 1990.

Yutang, L., ed. *The Wisdom of China and India*. New York: Random House, 1942.

OTHER BOOKS FROM TUTTLE BY ANNELLEN AND C. ALEXANDER SIMPKINS

PRINCIPLES OF MEDITATION

Eastern Wisdom for the Western Mind

Simple exercises train the mind for meditation, which can be used for relaxation, focus, and habit control.

0-8048-3074-6 • US $16.95 • pb

LIVING MEDITATION

From Principle to Practice

Useful and direct ways of applying meditation to improve your life. Through simple exercises learn to break bad habits, improve your memory, and balance your emotions.

0-8048-3114-9 • US $16.95 • pb

ZEN AROUND THE WORLD

A 2500-Year Journey from the Buddha to You

The Simpkins bring traditional Buddhist legends to life, helping readers understand the spirit of Zen.

0-8048-3082-7 • US $21.95 • pb

THE TUTTLE LIBRARY
OF ENLIGHTENMENT

BEYOND SANITY AND MADNESS
The Way of Zen Master Dogen
by Dennis Genpo Merzel
The teachings of Dogen Zenji through commentaries on three of Dogen's most significant works.
0-8048-3035-5 • US $14.95 • pb

THE BUTTERFLY'S DREAM
In Search of the Roots of Zen
by Albert Low
Reveals the roots of Zen spirituality and shows them to be as much Western as they are Eastern.
0-8048-1822-3 • US $14.95 • pb

FREE YOURSELF OF EVERYTHING
Radical Guidance in the Spirit of Zen and Christian Mysticism
by Wolfgang Kopp
Guides the reader step-by-step along the spiritual way.
0-8048-1989-0 • US $12.95 • pb

FUNDAMENTALS OF MAINSTREAM BUDDHISM
by Eric Cheetham
Presents the major topics of the first phase of Indian Buddhism. Prepared by the distinguished Buddhist Society of London.
0-8048-3008-8 • US $16.95 • pb

GOING BEYOND BUDDHA
The Awakening Practice of Listening
by Zen Master Dae Gak

Uses a refreshingly different metaphor for Zen—that of listening. It returns us to our true way—the way of compassion.

0-8048-3116-5 • US $18.95 • pb

THE HEART OF BEING
Moral and Ethical Teachings of Zen Buddhism
by John Daido Loori

Presents Buddhist teachings on a wide range of social and moral issues in the modern world.

0-8048-3078-9 • US $16.95 • pb

I CHING CLARIFIED
A Practical Guide
by Mondo Secter

Basic introduction and primer to the I Ching. Includes specially designed cards invented by the author. Calligraphy, charts, diagrams.

0-8048-1802-9 • US $14.95 • pb

THE STORY OF CHINESE ZEN
by Nan Huai-Chin
trans. by Thomas Cleary

To tell the story of Chinese Zen, Master Nan Huai-Chin looks to culture and history during the Han Dynasty and earlier.

0-8048-3050-9 • US $16.95 • pb

THE TAO OF ZEN
by Ray Grigg

First book which systemically links Taoism and Zen. Traces the evolution of Ch'an (Zen) in China and later in Japan.

0-8048-1988-2 • US $14.95 • pb

TO KNOW YOURSELF
Talks, Stories, and Articles on Zen

by Albert Low

Provides an engaging collection of articles, stories, and essays on Zen. Though the entries range from dharma talks on koans to discussions on Buddhism and Christianity, they all address concrete concerns of our lives and reveal the author's profound insights.

0-8048-3119-X • US $16.95 • pb

TWO ARROWS MEETING IN MID-AIR
The Zen Koan

by John Daido Loori

Koans from classic collections and modern encounters. Presents the relevance of koan study as it relates to Zen training today.

0-8048-3012-6 • US $16.95 • pb

UNDERSTANDING ZEN
by Benjamin Radcliff and Amy Radcliff

Zen is explained in a simple, straightforward way, drawing analogies to the mainstream of Western science and philosophy.

0-8048-1808-8 • US $14.95 • pb

THE WHOLE WORLD IS A SINGLE FLOWER
365 Kong-ans for Everyday Life

by Zen Master Seung Sahn

Includes koans from Chinese and Korean Zen, Lao-tzu, and the Christian tradition.

0-8048-1782-0 • US $16.95 • pb

THE WORLD: A GATEWAY
Commentaries on the Mumonkan

by Albert Low

The Mumonkan is the most widely used collection of koans in Zen practice. Includes contemporary commentaries on this great collection.

0-8048-3046-0 • US $16.95 • pb

ZEN BEYOND ALL WORDS
A Western Zen Master's Instructions
by Wolfgang Kopp
Teaches a direct and powerful Zen which leads to the enlightenment of the mind.
0-8048-3086-X • US $12.95 • pb

ZEN LIGHT
Unconventional Commentaries on the Denkoroku
by Stefano Mui Baragato, Sensei
0-8048-3106-8 • US $14.95 • pb

Look for all Tuttle books in your
local bookstore or call or write to:

Tuttle Publishing
RR1 Box 231-5
North Clarendon, VT 05759-9700

toll-free: 1-800-526-2778
phone: 802-773-8930